First published 2012 by Cornell University Press
Printed in the United States of America

Library of Congress Cataloging-in-Publication Data

Reich, Adam D. (Adam Dalton), 1981–
    With God on our side: the struggle for Workers' Rights
in a Catholic hospital / Adam D. Reich.
        p. cm. — (The culture and politics of health care work)
    Includes bibliographical references and index.
    ISBN 978-0-8014-5066-2 (cloth : alk. paper)
    1. Santa Rosa Memorial Hospital—Employees—Labor unions—
Organizing.   2. Catholic hospitals—Employees—Labor unions—
Organizing—California—Santa Rosa.   3. Labor movement—
California—Santa Rosa.   4. Labor—Religious aspects—Catholic
Church.   I. Title.   II. Series: Culture and politics of health care work.
    RA975.C37R445   2012
    362.11088—dc23   2011038541

Cornell University Press strives to use environmentally responsible suppliers and materials to the fullest extent possible in the publishing of its books. Such materials include vegetable-based, low-VOC v and acid-free papers that are recycled, totally chlorine-free, or partly composed of nonwood fibers. For further information, visit our website at www.cornellpress.cornell.edu.

Cloth printing   10 9 8 7 6 5 4 3 2 1

For Teresa

Contents

PREFACE

I was out of bed by three in the morning and in Fred Ross Jr.'s station wagon a little after four. Fred Ross Jr. is in his sixties, tall and thin with a dimpled chin. His father, Fred Ross Sr., mentored Cesar Chavez in the early days of the United Farm Worker (UFW) movement. Fred Ross Jr. became a labor organizer with the UFW straight out of college and has spent his life working for a better world in a variety of capacities. In 1975 he led the largest UFW action in a decade, a twenty-thousand-person march from San Francisco to Modesto as part of a successful campaign to pass the Agricultural Labor Relations Act. The law, passed by the California Legislature later that year, was the first in the nation to give farm workers collective bargaining rights, such as the right to organize a union and obtain a contract.[1] In the 1980s, Ross directed a coffee boycott that helped to end U.S. support for the brutal military government in El Salvador. In the 1990s he was Congresswoman Nancy Pelosi's chief of staff in California, before joining with other UFW alumni to lead an immigrant rights campaign. And on this cold and foggy morning when I joined the United Healthcare Workers West, Service Employees International Union (SEIU-UHW) for the first day of a big strike at California Pacific Medical Center in San Francisco in the early fall of 2005, Ross had been working for SEIU's hospital division for six years.

Fred Ross Jr. and Eileen Purcell, his colleague at the international union, were charged with developing the union's Catholic hospital strategy. They were both Catholics themselves, and together they were a dynamic duo, a community organizer's dream team. In the 1980s, Purcell had co-founded the Sanctuary movement for Central American refugees and the National Sanctuary Defense Fund, working especially with the people of El Salvador as they sought to rebuild their lives in the midst of the country's civil war. Before Ross recruited her to SEIU, Purcell had been the executive director of the SHARE Foundation, which also supported organizing efforts by the people of El Salvador. In these roles Purcell forged close and lasting relationships with many religious leaders in the United States and abroad.

Ross's history with the UFW, his leadership of the coffee boycott through Neighbor-2-Neighbor, his extensive political experience, and his law degree mean that he has credibility in almost all aspects of the organizing world. He can rile up a crowd of cafeteria workers as easily as he can build a relationship with a priest or convince a senator to sign a letter. Several workers and organizers have also had the experience of meeting Fred Ross Jr., esquire, when they have been harassed or arrested by the police during an action. Ross often serves as in-street lawyer. Purcell, meanwhile, is able to straddle the worlds of organized labor, international politics, and religion with grace and aplomb—and she is the only organizer I've ever met who has expressed her commitment to worker justice in a published psalm.[2]

As we drove across an empty San Francisco Bay Bridge into the city, Ross regaled me with stories of his days with the UFW. Cesar Chavez had told him to organize farm workers in Oregon, but Ross was hesitant. He had heard that Latinos in Oregon were insular, hostile even to Latinos from California, not to mention a gringo. But over time Ross was able to organize them, proving to himself that anyone can organize anyone else with the right skills. Organizing is a craft, he seemed to be telling me, that transcends an organizer's identity.

We pulled up to the hospital in San Francisco still well before dawn, and on this morning the only skills I put to use were my legs. A bus filled with replacement workers circled the hospital, and I tried to prove my chops by taking off after it. What I could do individually to stop a bus-load of people I wasn't sure. Fortunately, at each entrance where the bus stopped, a crowd of organizers and striking workers shouted, "Scabs, go home!" As a stocky redheaded man on staff of the union pounded on the door of the bus and forcibly prevented anyone from stepping off, the scene brought to mind the heyday of organized labor in the 1930s. And when the bus ultimately was forced to leave, I felt a surge of adrenaline, like *this* was union power at its essence.

Later that week, as the strike got into full swing, I came back to the hospital and—on the recommendation of a union staff person—pretended to be an expectant father concerned for the safety of my pregnant wife. In our fabricated story, my wife was scheduled to deliver at the hospital the following month. I was instructed to complain about the strike and to try to gather intelligence about what effect it was having on the floor. I complained my way to the nurse director of the obstetrics department before she asked me the name of my wife's obstetrician. I balked, then stammered that we didn't yet have one. The nurse called my bluff. She ordered me not to move and turned quickly away, while I sprinted down the hospital stairs and past a line of beefy security guards. I kept running away from the picket line until I was safely in my car and headed back to my apartment in Berkeley.

Three years later, almost to the day, I actually became a father. On a brisk October evening my wife Teresa gave birth to our daughter Ella at the Berkeley affiliate of the same hospital chain I had helped strike those years before. After a relatively smooth labor and delivery, and two dream-like days in a beautiful private room overlooking San Francisco Bay, we were about to go home when Ella spiked a fever of 101. The doctors were worried about a possible infection, and we were told that Ella would have to spend the next three days in the Neonatal Intensive Care Unit (NICU), where she would be hooked up to an IV, given large amounts of antibiotics, and monitored closely around the clock.

The NICU is a glistening shrine to modern medical technology. Premature babies of less than two pounds, who could never have made it fifty years ago, are incubated, respirated, and ushered into healthy and normal lives. But since most of the infants in the NICU are there long term, and many are seriously ill, the place feels sad and somewhat intimidating.

Nurses do their rounds accompanied by the blips and beeps of monitors, and as a whole don't seem to have much time for parents—who themselves are often compelled to return to something like regular life before their babies are healthy enough to return home, and so appear on the unit only sporadically.

But our case was different. If the tests came back okay, Ella had to be in the unit for only seventy-two hours. So Teresa and I spent those hours clinging to Ella as if she were a life preserver in a fierce sea, as we fought off the urge for sleep and the practical (if somewhat cursory) advice of nurses who thought we were being just a little too *Berkeley*.

Needless to say, Teresa and I nearly lost our minds. It was only thanks to a veteran nurse named Mildred that we stayed on this side of the brink. Mildred had been working at the hospital for almost three decades, and although she had already retired she still took the odd shift. With gentle humor she told us about her own kids, now grown, and warned us that our worries were just beginning—that we should thank our lucky stars Ella was far from being a teenager! She reassured us that Ella would be out of the hospital in no time, and made us feel taken care of amid the flurry and worry of the unit. When Ella's tests came back clear, we wept with gratitude for Mildred's small kindnesses, and she told us that these sorts of experiences were what kept her coming back to the hospital year after year.

These two stories illustrate for me the paradox of work in the hospital. In some ways the hospital is the modern factory, and labor organizing in the hospital is similar to organizing at any other large industrial workplace. In other ways, as Ella's birth brought home to me, the work that goes on in the hospital is loaded with emotion and meaning, giving struggle in the hospital a special character. This book explores in detail the tension between worker power and workers' emotional relationship to their work. For unions to be successful in the healthcare industry and beyond, they must combine an attention to power and control with an appreciation of the cultural context of work—and must link workers' political-economic interests with broader considerations of the public good.

Acknowledgments

This book tells the story of a group of worker leaders, union organizers, and religious allies who overcame countless obstacles to help workers win a union election at Santa Rosa Memorial Hospital, a Catholic hospital in the small city of Santa Rosa, California, about an hour north of San Francisco. These leaders' humor, wisdom, and deep commitment to social justice represent for me what is best about the modern U.S. labor movement. Without their courage and their persistence, there would be no story to tell. I am especially grateful that many of these leaders have been willing to participate in this book. Among them, most of whom I have promised confidentiality, I would like especially to recognize Fred Ross Jr. and Eileen Purcell, who served as my mentors and coaches over the course of my involvement in the campaign. I also owe tremendous debts to Glenn Goldstein and Peter Tappeiner, two organizers on the campaign and ongoing sources of inspiration. Jim Araby, a political organizer on the campaign and a close friend, has read several versions of this project and offered valuable feedback throughout. His breadth and depth of knowledge about the labor movement and about modern American politics has helped me immensely as I have tried to connect the lessons of Santa Rosa with the challenges facing the labor movement more generally. He has also been a steady source of moral support in the more difficult days of the writing process.

During my work on the campaign I came to know many religious and community leaders who supported workers in their unionization struggle and deserve special recognition. Monsignor John Brenkle, Father Angelito Peries, Father Ramon Pons, Reverend Blythe Sawyer, Reverend Chris Bell, JoAnn Consiglieri, and Stephen Harper are only some of the many leaders in Sonoma County whose ongoing work gives me hope that meaningful social change is possible.

The publication of a book, it turns out, is a kind of organizing project in itself. Throughout the process, Michael Burawoy has consistently offered a critical eye and supportive ear. He has read and edited countless drafts of the manuscript, but as importantly has encouraged me to pursue a life that balances scholarship with practice, a commitment out of which this book has emerged. Along the way, several other scholars have helped shepherd this project to publication, among them Kim Voss, Ruth Milkman, and Steve Early. Years of conversation with Marshall Ganz about the art and craft of organizing have also helped to inform this project.

At Cornell University Press, Fran Benson, Suzanne Gordon, and Sioban Nelson have been an especially remarkable group of editors with whom to work. Suzanne even came to Berkeley and helped me reshape my introduction in person, with both of us huddled over my laptop in a busy coffee shop. Thanks to Susan Specter and John Raymond for their attention to matters both large and small. The book is much stronger as a result of their editing. Thanks also to an anonymous reviewer solicited by the press who gave quite thorough and thoughtful feedback.

The roots of this project go back even further. My father, Robert Reich, has advocated on behalf of working people since before I was born. He is a role model as an engaged intellectual, not to mention a role model as a father. He was also an enthusiastic participant in the St. Joseph Health System campaign. My mother, Clare Dalton, is even more of a radical—first as a legal scholar and advocate for victims of intimate partner violence, and more recently as an acupuncturist. Her journey continues to inspire me to follow my own conscience, wherever it may lead. Thanks to both of them for changing my diapers, for feeding me, and for giving me the right values.

Finally, I would like to thank Teresa Sharpe, my partner, to whom I have dedicated this book. Teresa's own work on the labor movement demonstrated to me how one might balance one's social justice commitments with careful analysis and critique. The first time we met for lunch, over burritos on Berkeley's campus, she shared with me her experiences working for a union while attending graduate school, and encouraged me to do the same. And as our friendship blossomed into marriage and into parenthood, she and I have continued to wrestle with broader questions about worker power and the cultural significance of work—that is, when we're not wrestling with our toddler, Ella.

A Note on Names

Social scientists face complicated ethical questions about the degree of anonymity they provide the subjects of their research. For many historians, time has given the events they describe a distance that allows for specificity. Sociologists writing about events closer at hand often occlude the people and places about which they write, creating a different kind of distance between readers and the experiences about which they are reading.

Neither of these solutions felt available to me. The events described in this book are still "raw" to many of the people who experienced them, as one respondent put it. Were I to wait for time to scab over the wounds, I might be waiting a very long time indeed. Yet the specifics of the campaign felt important to the lessons I was able to draw from it. Moreover, I wanted to recognize the successes of workers at Santa Rosa Memorial Hospital and those who worked alongside them.

In order to balance my commitment to specificity with my ethical obligations as a researcher, I have compromised. The people in the text identified by their full names are either interviewees who agreed to be identified, or people who were publicly identified in media accounts of the Santa Rosa Memorial Hospital campaign. Those identified by first names only are participants who appear regularly in the story but whose names I have changed in order to protect their anonymity. Those participants in the study who appear only sporadically I have identified by position alone.

Abbreviations

AFL-CIO	American Federation of Labor and Congress of Industrial Organizations
AFSCME	American Federation of State, County and Municipal Employees
CHA	Catholic Health Association of the United States
CHW	Catholic Healthcare West
CNA	California Nurses Association
HERE	Hotel Employees and Restaurant Employees International Union
NLRA	National Labor Relations Act
NLRB	National Labor Relations Board
NUHW	National Union of Healthcare Employees
SEIU	Service Employees International Union
SEIU-UHW	Service Employees International Union, United Healthcare Workers West
SJHS	St. Joseph Health System

SRMH	Santa Rosa Memorial Hospital
UAW	United Auto Workers
UFW	United Farm Workers
UNITE	Union of Needletrades, Industrial and Textile Employees
USCCB	United States Conference of Catholic Bishops

WITH GOD ON OUR SIDE

INTRODUCTION

Work's Meaning and Labor's Power

Santa Rosa Memorial Hospital (SRMH) is nestled in a residential neighborhood a few blocks away from downtown Santa Rosa, an exurban community about an hour north of San Francisco. Even with the prominent blue "H" hospital signs leading the way, the hospital can be difficult to find for an out-of-towner. A statue of St. Joseph, the earthly father of Jesus, welcomes visitors at the hospital's main entrance, and an old convent, long ago converted into administrative offices, sits adjacent to the facility, a buffer between the hospital and the surrounding community.

Since its founding in 1950, the hospital has been owned by the Sisters of St. Joseph of Orange, a group of nuns who preside over thirteen hospitals in California, New Mexico, and Texas that together make up the not-for-profit St. Joseph Health System (SJHS). Although these Sisters were once actively involved in nursing and administration at Memorial Hospital, their numbers have become too small and too elderly to maintain an active presence there. Yet they still actively govern the health system as a whole and still work to infuse each of their facilities with the values they see as central to hospital care.[1]

The Sisters of St. Joseph of Orange are widely regarded as one of the most progressive orders of nuns in the state, if not the country. Not only were they among the first sisters in the United States to abandon the habit but they actively supported Cesar Chavez and the United Farm Workers throughout the 1960s and 1970s. Several spent time in a Fresno jail with grape strikers in the summer of 1973. Much to the dismay of these same Sisters, workers at Santa Rosa Memorial Hospital spent more than six years trying to organize a union.

In this book I follow workers' union organizing efforts at Santa Rosa Memorial Hospital between 2004 and 2010. In 2004 and 2005, workers and union leaders attempted to organize within the standard framework of the federal National Labor Relations Board (NLRB). Yet in the face of a concerted and sophisticated antiunion campaign led by management and supported by the hospital's religious leadership, workers and union leaders were forced to withdraw from this election in the face of imminent defeat. The campaign then became more open-ended as the union sought what it termed a "fair election agreement," a set of ground rules and accountability mechanisms that would limit the hospital's antiunion practices. In this effort workers and union leaders organized in the political and religious communities in new ways. Between 2007 and 2008, the union built a community coalition that sought to link the Memorial campaign with the county's broader healthcare crisis. Although the coalition was unsuccessful in its narrower political goals, it was an important part of the union's broader project. Between 2005 and 2009, the union built a powerful religious and political coalition to highlight the contradictions between the values the hospital asserted and its antiunion practices, a project that *did* win important concessions from the hospital corporation in the fall of 2008. At the very moment of greatest hope, however, the union was thrown into disarray by an internecine labor dispute. When workers finally voted on unionization in December 2010, they did so with few resources and *in opposition to* the Service Employees International Union (SEIU), the organization that had helped to initiate the campaign.

Throughout this process workers faced intimidation and harassment from their supervisors, from hospital administrators, and ultimately from the members and leadership of an opposition union. As important, workers had to reconcile their desire for more power and voice in their workplace with their vocational commitments to their patients. The obstacles these workers faced, and their ultimate success, make the organizing drive at Santa Rosa Memorial Hospital a crucible within which to examine the challenges and possibilities facing labor unions in service industries across the country.

The Hospital, the Union, and the Twenty-First-Century Workplace

Today's healthcare sector is one of the largest industries in the United States, employing 14.3 million people, approximately 35 percent of whom work in hospitals.[2] The hospital has replaced the factory as the main source of employment in many communities. In cities such as Rochester, Minnesota, and Cleveland, Ohio, well-known centers of medical practice and innovation overshadow the manufacturing industries the hospitals were first constructed to serve. Catholic hospitals are a major player in this industry. In 2009 there were fifty-nine Catholic health systems that together provided almost 15 percent of all hospital care in the United States.[3]

Hospital work has also, in some ways, come to resemble work in the large unionized workplaces of the mid-twentieth century. The fiefdoms of midcentury hospital work have given way to integrated hierarchical organizations that have made even doctors feel less like professionals and more like wage earners. Medical specialization and fragmentation have diminished the importance of the physician-patient relationship by introducing new technologies and new delivery systems that divide treatment into its component parts.[4] Unlike manufacturing industries, which have moved production offshore in the face of high labor costs, hospitals cannot as easily transfer operations to places where labor is cheaper, nor can they as easily replace labor power with technology. The workforce is fairly centralized and fairly integrated. And as financial pressures increase in the industry, many workers are being squeezed by being asked to work more hours and take on more responsibilities without commensurate increases in pay.

Finally, far from ushering in a free market of relatively autonomous and competitive buyers and sellers, the corporate transformation of the

U.S. healthcare system has been accompanied by large-scale processes of *organizing* by the market's constituent parts.[5] Hospitals have merged in order to negotiate better rates with insurers and physicians, physicians have organized groups in order to negotiate better rates with hospitals and insurance companies, and all three groups have sometimes merged (into health maintenance organizations or preferred provider organizations) in order to negotiate with employers and individual patients. All of these constituencies have used principles of combination to increase their economic leverage with the others.

In these ways the hospital seems a natural site for labor organizing, representing a glimmer of hope in the face of labor's forty-year decline across the private sector.[6] In other ways, however, the hospital is strikingly different from those workplaces in which the labor movement was born. Since workers in not-for-profit hospitals were first excluded from the protections of the National Labor Relations Act as part of the Taft-Hartley Act of 1947, hospital work has been distinguished legally from other sorts of labor. Not only were hospitals primarily oriented around noneconomic values, it was argued, and so inappropriate targets for unionization, but they were also dealing with matters of life and death, making the threat of work disruption dangerous and immoral.[7] Even after the protections of the NLRA again were extended to hospital workers in 1974, the law has sought to balance the rights of hospital workers against the rights of the public to uninterrupted hospital care.

If hospital work was the anomaly at midcentury, in 2010 it is representative of the interactive care work so prevalent in today's U.S. economy. The future for American labor seems likely to hinge on its success in industries like health care: industries that orient themselves at least in part toward public goods; industries in which workers' values and emotional lives are closely entangled with their jobs. Even public sector employees such as teachers and social service workers, recently regarded as the last bastion of U.S. unionism,[8] have found their political and bureaucratic sources of power coming under increasing attack, and must identify new sources of power and legitimacy. The lessons that can be learned from an analysis of hospital organizing have implications far beyond the hospital's walls.

These lessons have implications outside the labor movement as well. Healthcare workers, teachers, social service workers, and other service-sector employees are often those in closest contact with the patients, students, and clients they serve. A revitalized labor movement can and must be closely linked to the protection and revitalization of patient care, student learning, and the public good. Union membership is one of the few mechanisms that allow workers to advocate on behalf of the constituencies they serve without fear of reprisal.[9]

Most broadly, this book explores the relationship between vocational values and worker power in the contemporary hospital and beyond. More specifically, it addresses three questions. First, how do hospital workers understand the noneconomic dimensions of their work, and how do these noneconomic values relate to their participation in labor unions? Second, in a context in which confrontational politics is understood by multiple constituencies as anathema to organizational mission, what should be the character of labor *struggle*? How can workers successfully challenge their disempowerment when this challenge is itself construed as inappropriate?[10] And finally, how do these two dimensions of labor struggle—workers' noneconomic values and the ideological face of the corporation—complicate existing debates about labor's power both on the shop floor and in the political arena?

Throughout this book, I argue that for unions to remain relevant in the hospital industry and beyond—winning support among workers, winning campaigns against employers, and winning broad-based political power—they must recognize the cultural dimension of labor struggle, and must be concerned as much with putting forward a vision of the public good as with winning material advantage. The campaign at Santa Rosa Memorial Hospital—and its relationship to broader successes and failures in the labor movement—illustrates the possibilities and perils of this approach to labor struggle.

Case and Methods

I focus on Santa Rosa Memorial Hospital because it epitomizes the values-based not-for-profit employer. Although vocational ethics infuse many care contexts, they are perhaps nowhere more prominent than in the Catholic hospital, where these ethics are articulated explicitly in the form of religious values. When I asked the deacon of a local church why it mattered whether or not a hospital was Catholic, he responded: "You ever been scared? . . . There isn't any time in the world when religion makes more sense than when you have a problem, especially a health problem, or [are] confronting death." A lead organizer in the union told me that these religious values are "often deeply felt by the workers." This is not to say that workers are necessarily religious themselves, but rather that the religious mission of the hospital resonates with their experience of the noneconomic aspects of their work. According to Sioban Nelson, a professor of nursing, workers want "to provide healthcare to all in their facilities with the highest respect and dignity for the patient and their families." People "feel good about those missions." Nelson documents how Catholic nuns established modern nursing "as a hybrid religious and professional practice."[11] This legacy lives on in the way that many workers relate to hospital work, perhaps most acutely in those hospitals founded by Catholic nuns.

It was Fred Ross Jr. who brought me up to Santa Rosa for the first time in the spring of 2006. As a first-year graduate student in sociology at UC Berkeley, I was interested in learning more about the theory and practice of labor organizing, and made a deal with myself to keep one foot in the world of practice. Like any good organizer, Ross wasn't satisfied with just one foot, and he suggested that I become one of the union's religious organizers. So over the next year and a half I worked about fifteen hours a week for the union, building relationships with local religious leaders, introducing them to hospital workers, and asking them to support the campaign in various ways. No matter that I was a nonpracticing Jew whose religious experience was limited to bar and bat mitzvahs and the occasional High Holy Days.

Throughout my involvement with the campaign I took detailed field notes, oftentimes reluctantly, as my world of practice had come temporarily to overshadow my academic ambitions. When I dove back into graduate work more wholeheartedly, between February 2009 and October 2010, I conducted open-ended interviews with worker leaders, union organizers, religious leaders, and hospital administrators and executives.

This book also makes use of a rich body of primary documents produced by both union and management over the course of the campaign. These include strategic memos written by union staff; public memos from the hospital administration to workers; flyers both for and against the union that were distributed to workers at the hospital; public advertisements taken out by both union and administration in local media outlets; media stories on the struggle; correspondence between union representatives and hospital administrators; correspondence between union representatives and religious and community leaders; and several "reports" produced by the union that were part of its campaign to gain public support. Perhaps most useful of all was a report produced at the culmination of the campaign by Eileen Purcell, a leader of SEIU's Catholic hospital strategy, which was intended to illustrate the campaign's successes and failures.[12]

My comparative case studies of different periods in the campaign to unionize Santa Rosa Memorial Hospital help us understand the important role that cultural ideas and broad-based organizing play for unionization efforts in the healthcare industry, and the possibilities for this sort of struggle throughout the modern labor movement.[13]

Workers and the Union: The Power to Care

The scholarship on service work has tended to treat emotional investment in work as something produced by corporations themselves. In her path-breaking study of airline attendants and bill collectors, the sociologist Arlie Hochschild studied what happens when workers' emotions become part of the commodity being sold.[14] The attendants, she found, were trained to feel nurturing, cheerful, and flirtatious on the job. Hochschild compared this learning of a role to Constantin Stanislavski's method of "deep acting."[15] Emotion work succeeded as a service to the extent, and only to the extent, that it was perceived as being "real." When workers' emotional lives were made a part of the product being sold, Hochschild argued, workers' experiences of alienation—and the possibilities for workers' resistance to it—were short circuited. Rachel Sherman pushed this line of inquiry even further in her study of workers at luxury hotels.[16] She found that the relationships workers had with hotel patrons became important to workers' senses of self, helping them feel equal to (and in some senses superior to) their affluent customers. Moreover, Sherman argued that workers' different access to these relationships created distinctions among them that undermined the potential for organized resistance. Although these "class acts" were somewhat illusory, given that workers were still structurally less powerful than the clients they served, they were experienced as real and important.

The meaning that healthcare employees attribute to their work as they help patients make sense of profound fear and uncertainty is difficult to dismiss as part of a commodity produced by hospital administrators. Workers take pride in their capacity to feel empathy for and provide assistance to vulnerable patients. And the results of their work—the physical and emotional well-being of patients—is also of real importance to healthcare workers. It is more immediately manifest to healthcare workers than it is to those making widgets on the assembly line, and of more significance than the contentment of passengers in airplanes or the well-being of patrons in hotels. The hospital worker may not be in control of the rhythm of his or her work. He or she may struggle to make ends meet. But this worker is often profoundly invested in the wellness of patients and so feels a sense of connection to the work itself and to the hospital within which it takes place.

In other words, the way that workers make sense of hospital work is embedded in their interactions with patients and is not merely a product of the corporation.[17] For Hochschild, emotions were "engineered and administered by large organizations."[18] Workers' identification with their work, then, meant that they were estranged from that most personal aspect of themselves. In an illuminating turn of phrase she called this phenomenon "the managed heart."

But if workers' emotional investments in work might have autonomy from management—as they seem to have in the hospital—we can identify *other* ways in which these investments might also affect workers' power on the job.[19] First, emotional investment with work might become a reason *not* to protest unfairness—the *martyred heart*. Paula England and her colleagues have shown that "care work" is devalued and underpaid in our culture. They suggest that the meaning workers attribute to this work may be at least part of the explanation for the devaluation, since "if the marginal worker sees the intrinsic properties of the work as an amenity, this permits a lower wage."[20] One's identification with one's work may come to be seen as replacing a part of one's wage—or one may feel so identified with one's workplace that one is willing to subordinate oneself to the organization for the "good of the whole." Second, identification with work might be understood *as* resistance to hospital leadership—the *misrecognized heart*. Workers may experience their own caring as reclaiming the noneconomic parts of their work from impersonal market pressures or bureaucratic imperatives. The paradox of this strategy, of course, is that it benefits the very organization from whose leadership workers feel estranged. Like those workers in sociologist Michael Burawoy's *Manufacturing Consent* who "make out" by increasing their own productivity, caring can be experienced as resistance at the same time that it boosts the hospital's reputation and bottom line.[21]

Finally, identification with work might become a reason to advocate for oneself, one's co-workers, one's capacity to do one's work well, and thus for one's patients—the *mobilized heart*. Workers may conclude that the only way they will be able to deliver the standard of care to which they are committed is to increase their own power within the organization as a whole. Because of the lack of protections afforded by U.S. labor law, workers who are not in unions are "employees at will" and can be fired summarily, without "just cause." The First Amendment's guarantees of free speech do not apply to the workplace and workers who want to advocate for their patients can be fired or disciplined without legal recourse. In nonunion workplaces, employers have no obligation to talk with workers about their concerns or bargain with them about working conditions that are connected to patient care. The only protected speech in the American workplace is what is known as "protected concerted activity," which is what unions provide.

All of which is to say, when workers in hospitals consider unionization, they do not merely weigh how a union will affect their economic position, although this is certainly a factor. They also take into account the degree to which a union will let them have a say in the way that the hospital takes care of its patients, and the extent to which a union will enable them to express (or prevent them from expressing) the noneconomic values that are central to the way they think about their work. In order to be successful, then, labor unions must engage with the cultural dimensions of hospital work, and they must help workers interpret their own participation in the union as being consistent with their own emotional commitment to their work.

In the first stage of the Santa Rosa Memorial Hospital campaign, worker leaders and union representatives treated the campaign as a struggle that was nearly indistinguishable from campaigns in other industries. After workers contacted SEIU-UHW in 2004, union representatives helped to develop an organizing committee of worker leaders and community supporters. Throughout this process the union sought to build what sociologist Rick Fantasia calls a "culture of solidarity" among workers that could overcome a market-driven management style.[22] Fantasia's rich case study of an organizing campaign among hospital workers in Springfield, Vermont, demonstrates the ways in which organizing committees can "provide an area of social space within the employer-dominated workplace where an alternative definition of social relations and power can be provided and maintained."[23] In Fantasia's success story, a culture emerged among union activists "with opposition as its central, defining feature."[24]

Yet this strategy was not enough at Santa Rosa Memorial Hospital, for two reasons. Most unsurprisingly, the very imbalance of power that union supporters sought to rectify through unionization meant that hospital management controlled the environment in which the union election was to take place. Managers intimidated workers, spread misinformation, and selectively raised wages in anticipation of the election. The uneven playing field during the election process, combined with a weak and loosely enforced labor law, meant that the union and its supporters were at a distinct disadvantage, as unions are throughout the country.[25]

But while hospital administrators stuck to standard antiunion strategies and tropes throughout this initial campaign, their underlying message also had a powerful impact on workers. The union was cast as an economically interested third party that would undermine the hospital's mission. In actuality, the local and international unions had already established productive partnerships with management at both Catholic Healthcare West (CHW), the largest Catholic health system in California, and at Kaiser Permanente, a large integrated managed care organization also based in California. At the workplace and at the political level, the union had worked with these hospital systems on shared goals, from healthcare reform and immigrant rights to patient ratios for non-RNs and procedures to prevent workplace injuries. Moreover, union leaders had met with the leadership of Saint Joseph Health System before any organizing began to explore the possibility of *avoiding* a protracted and adversarial unionization campaign. These conversations had gone nowhere, however, and union leaders concluded that the health system would not dialogue without feeling some pressure. But SJHS consistently interpreted this pressure as a kind of symbolic violence, and this interpretation played powerfully into some workers' hesitation about the union. The oppositional culture of solidarity fostered among union organizers and worker leaders was effectively portrayed by the hospital as something that threatened workers' capacity to care for their patients.

The limits of oppositional politics may be especially apparent in the healthcare context, but these limits are likely more general. Research suggests that while a majority of U.S. workers do want some say over how their workplace is organized, and do see the value in collective representation over issues of wages and working conditions, most do *not* want the adversarial relationship with their employer that they worry a union entails.[26] The paradoxical question, then, is, how can unions win power and voice for workers without this struggle being *understood* as conflictual?

Fantasia's oppositional solidarity fails to take into consideration the deep emotional relationship many hospital workers have with their work—an investment that makes certain kinds of conflict especially uncomfortable. His attention to workers' understandings and practices is critically important, yet his case study of hospital workers sits alongside studies of workers in the steel-casting and corn-processing industries, implying that labor and capital (and the struggle between them) can be understood similarly in these different contexts. That is, while Fantasia is careful to discuss the plural "*cultures* of solidarity" in order to "afford analysis of discrete case studies of collective actions,"[27] nevertheless he seems to describe a particular type of process common across his cases—a process in which workers move from alienation to collectivity, from estrangement to solidarity, establishing autonomous "cultural formations that arise in conflict, creating and sustaining solidarity in opposition to the dominant structure."[28] Even scholars who grapple more deeply with the particular nature of healthcare work argue along similar lines. The sociologist Paul Johnston recognizes what he calls "the dilemma of autonomy and care"[29] among nurses, but suggests that nurses' "self-assertion" through unionization "implies turning away from the 'Florence Nightingale' attitude and demanding respect, fair pay, and the right 'to take care of myself'."[30] He does not interrogate the conditions under which unionization can come to be seen as *enhancing* the capacity to care.

The prototypical example of labor's oppositional solidarity is the strike, or the collective withdrawal of labor power. Yet given the high stakes of hospital care, many hospital workers are reluctant to strike, worrying about the effects of the strike on those for whom they would otherwise be responsible.[31] In order to feel comfortable challenging power relationships within the hospital, then, workers need to embrace the *mobilized heart*— they need to feel that supporting the union is consistent with the hospital's larger mission of patient care. As a lead organizer at Santa Rosa Memorial Hospital put the point, "You have to organize people to a vision of good."

Scholars have long recognized the limits of adversarial politics within the healthcare industry and service sector more generally.[32] It is no surprise, then, that a theme of almost every antiunion campaign—in healthcare as well as in other helping services—is that unions represent interests *opposed* to the well-being of patients or clients. In an emblematic article, the medical scholars Christopher Bryan-Brown and Kathleen Dracup write that unions "tend to destroy the ideals of professionalism because they are not patient centered. Unions generally look askance at altruistic behavior and at the professional who wishes to go the extra mile for a patient."[33] The article argues that healthcare workers often operate in environments of resource scarcity: "Making the best we can with what we have is a more certain professional approach than trying to get a better deal through a trade union."[34] In what has become an almost classic confusion, the authors here conflate professionalism and sacrifice, and assume that workers' interests are identical with the interests of the health systems for which they work. Unions and workers do not protest going the "extra mile for patients," but rather resist running workplace marathons for large employers on behalf of these corporations' bottom lines. Moreover, preliminary studies of the relationship between unionization and patient outcomes demonstrate positive effects of a unionized workforce on patient care. For example, mortality rates of cardiac patients have been found to be lower in unionized hospitals than in their nonunion counterparts.[35] Presumably, unionized workers were better able to point out patient care problems without fear of reprisal.

The perception that unions are enemies of altruism is at least in part a product of the narrowness of American labor law (about which authors like Bryan-Brown and Dracup often seem woefully ignorant), which limits the scope of mandatory bargaining to wages, hours, and working conditions. In the United States, antiunion ideology has become so pervasive that authors like Bryan-Brown and Dracup see negative effects even in such patient safety initiatives as staffing ratios that have been promoted by unions.[36] They claim that staffing ratios are actually harmful to patients as a whole, since these ratios are incompatible with "a worldwide shortfall in the number of nurses needed to maintain the ratios."[37] This analysis overlooks that the pay and conditions of healthcare work are important causes of staff shortages, and that these conditions are exactly what unions help to ameliorate. Yet the popular conception of unions as narrowly interested, self-serving, and undermining of vocational values is hard to shake—even among some workers themselves.

The Union and the Hospital: The Struggle over Catholic Teaching

In the face of their initial setback, union organizers and worker leaders regrouped and decided to wage a public, community campaign for what it called a "fair election agreement": a set of ground rules and accountability mechanisms that would limit the hospital's antiunion campaign and create an environment in which workers could "freely" choose whether they wanted a union. As unions across the country have struggled against concerted management opposition and a weak labor law, these sorts of longer-term campaigns—campaigns over the process by which workers choose—have become more common.[38] And as it sought to pressure the employer to agree to such ground rules, the union engaged in strategies typical of "social movement unionism," finding sources of leverage in the political arena, in the media, and among religious leaders and community coalitions.[39]

Ultimately, however, the union campaign at Santa Rosa Memorial Hospital became a struggle over the meaning and implications of Catholic teaching. According to the union and its supporters, the religious values on which the hospital was founded had been corroded by the healthcare market. The hospital system's espousal of Catholic values was hypocritical, corporate mumbo-jumbo. Indeed, since the 1970s, the "values-driven" approach to management has become increasingly common among corporations of all stripes. For example, Starbucks advertises that "Working at Starbucks is a lot like working with your friends." Walmart has a slogan, "A career at Walmart is more than a job. It's a way to ignite your spark."[40] Even earlier in the twentieth century, personnel departments had been aware of the ways in which promoting company values could inspire loyalty, discourage collective action, and—to paraphrase the title of a book by the antiunion industrial psychologist Charles L. Hughes—*make unions feel unnecessary*.[41] For supporters of the union, St. Joseph Health System was merely using its religious legacy to rationalize worker exploitation and subjugation.

Even though the Sisters of St. Joseph of Orange had long since turned over hospital management to laypeople, the Sisters still controlled the governing board of the system, and had asserted on numerous occasions that they were the primary decision makers. According to the union and their allies, then, the Sisters were risking their legacy by sanctioning aggressive antiunion tactics, since Catholic social teaching required that the hospital be supportive of unionization.

The Sisters and their hired ethicist agreed with the union about the importance of a dignified workplace but argued that unions were only one way of achieving it. Moreover, they suggested, a union would undermine the hospitals' "Biblical community." And just as the union regarded the system as hiding behind theological rhetoric, the Sisters saw the union's invocation of Catholic teaching as part of a strategic "corporate campaign" that assaulted the image of the hospital system, manipulating workers and community allies alike to join the union's cause. The union's use of theology was purely instrumental, hospital leaders claimed, one weapon in an arsenal that was designed to bring about what the antiunion political scientist Jarol Manheim characterized as a *death of a thousand cuts*.[42]

Although the union drew on a rich tradition of Catholic social teaching on the rights of workers to organize, the hospital leadership had important sources of cultural power as well. The Sisters of St. Joseph of Orange were not only owners of the hospital but also traditionally had been the hospital's moral leaders, embodying and supporting employees' vocational commitment to care. As nuns, they represented an ethic of subordinated femininity—a life of self-sacrifice and religious identification. Even without evangelizing their religious beliefs among the workforce, they fostered among workers a similar ethic of selflessness and self-sacrifice. These Sisters were acting with precedent. In the 1930s and 1940s, the Catholic Health Association struck an alliance with the American Hospital Association over the status of hospital workers in the recently minted National Labor Relations Act. Together these groups sought exemption from the act on the grounds that "low pay was a virtue, since it attracted staff who were motivated by the 'right values.'"[43] The role of Catholic hospitals was essential to this argument because "it extended, by analogy, the dedicated service of Roman Catholic nuns to the jobs of all hospital workers."[44]

For the union to win an election agreement with St. Joseph Health System it would have to engage the Sisters on the ethical terrain the Sisters saw as central to their ministry. And given the Sisters' moral commitments, they reacted to economic and political pressure in unexpected ways. A lead organizer in the campaign to organize Santa Rosa Memorial Hospital explained that organizing in the for-profit hospital industry was simpler than organizing most Catholic hospitals. He said that for-profit companies "have a clear objective, they want to make as much money as possible," and would capitulate if the union caused them to lose enough money. Catholic systems, however, "have an ethic," and the sisters who own these hospitals believe that they are "good advocates" for their workers. Sisters understand unionization as an indictment of their leadership, he suggested, and so are ideologically opposed to unionization even when it makes economic sense to settle.

The union's success on this terrain was due, in large part, to its capacity to *combine* a concern with power with a concern for values; to combine collective action with dialogue and deep relationships; and to combine workers' involvement and workers' voices with dialogue and debate among Catholic leaders at the national level. The Sisters of St. Joseph of Orange had natural theological legitimacy as women who had dedicated their lives to religious practice and care giving. And while many union leaders rooted their work in religious traditions as well, the union was more vulnerable to having its relationship to theological teaching be dismissed as instrumental. For the union's theological position to be taken seriously within the religious community, then, union leaders had to navigate the tension between their moral commitments and their organizational goals—between authenticity and instrumentality.[45]

Despite the diversity in the literature on contemporary labor unions, no existing scholarship adequately explains this cultural terrain on which the labor struggle ultimately was fought. This is because the literature is limited by materialist assumptions, and tends to paint employers as one-dimensional market actors motivated by the bottom line alone. Even for those who articulate most powerfully the importance of moral or cultural resources to union drives, the dominant narrative has been one of leveraging moral arguments *against* market forces, be they agribusiness companies or multinational hotels.[46] Religious and cultural traditions are understood as tools that help motivate workers and their allies fight back against an impersonal capitalist adversary.

Although labor scholars have tended, with some notable exceptions, to underestimate the role of culture in contemporary labor struggles, social movement scholarship has engaged with the question of culture through the concept of "framing."[47] Frames are "action-oriented sets of beliefs and meanings that inspire and legitimate the activities and campaigns of a social movement organization,"[48] and thus "mediate between structural parameters and . . . social actors."[49] Recently, the sociologist Marc Steinberg has pushed this line of analysis even further by suggesting that we understand framing as taking place in a "discursive field" within which multiple sides work to legitimate their interpretation of these symbols to a broader audience.[50] The goal of a social movement organization is not so much to create an oppositional culture as to win legitimacy over the symbols at stake.[51]

This theoretical orientation allows us to investigate the process by which the union engaged in ideological struggle with St. Joseph Health System. Importantly, *each* side argued that it represented a vision of Catholic teaching in the face of impersonal market forces embodied by the other, and each side struggled with the inconsistencies and contradictions in its orientation. For the union, the immorality of the market was reflected in the unequal power relationships the market tended to create; Catholic teaching has long asserted the rights of workers to organize for exactly this reason. For the Sisters, the immorality of the market was reflected in its tendency to depersonalize and commodify social relationships; Catholic teaching asserted the dignity of the worker, which—hospital leaders argued—under some circumstances actually might be undermined by a bureaucratic and impersonal union structure. In this way each subscribed to a view of the market as fundamentally immoral, yet each side identified the immorality of the market in the *other*. The conflict took on the qualities of a Rubin's vase, with each side seeing the market in the other without seeing it in itself.

Cultural Struggle

The workers' relationship to the union and the union's cultural struggle with St. Joseph Health System may be analytically distinct, but they are deeply intertwined. The moral legitimacy of the Sisters within the Catholic hospital helped to instill among workers the *martyred heart*. One oft-repeated story among union supporters in the Santa Rosa Memorial Hospital campaign was how a nun had approached a prounion worker and told her she was "greedy" for wanting a union. Although the message was rarely so explicit, workers were consistently reminded of the vocational nature of their work and urged to mirror the Sisters' own selflessness. The theological campaign over the rights of workers to organize simultaneously helped workers feel that their involvement with the union was consistent with the hospital's mission.

Values became an important terrain of struggle, then, not only because of the hospital's religious legacy and religious leadership but also because these religious values resonated with workers' sense of the noneconomic dimension to the care they provided. The organizing work undertaken by the union thus had an impact both on the context within which the election was to take place and on the beliefs and understandings of the workers who would ultimately choose whether to unionize. What began as a battle over positional power in the organization became one over the values underlying it.

This is not to say that unions should abandon bread-and-butter concerns—far from it. Rather, in a context in which the meaning of work matters, both for workers themselves and within the wider political context of struggle, unions must think carefully about how to weave together economic and cultural power. This endeavor must go beyond discursive processes of "framing" to infuse union practice as well. As a simple example, in the context of health care, unions must make clear how workers' interests are in keeping with patients' interests as well. One organizer described with a pained look on her face a decision made several years ago by the union to picket the opening of an acute-care clinic at a union-busting hospital system.

This vision for U.S. unionism is quite consistent with the theory articulated by Antonio Gramsci in his *Prison Notebooks*.[52] For Gramsci, revolutionary change was contingent on workers and intellectuals putting forward a vision of the social world in which workers' interests were in the interests of the entire society. Workers had to move from solidarity based on similar work, and even from solidarity based on class position, to an "intellectual and moral unity"[53] that would make working-class power consistent with a broader vision of the social good. There are echoes of

Gramsci in the way that Eileen Purcell, a union leader in the St. Joseph Health System campaign, described her own vision for the labor movement: "I'm about building unions that are knitting together relationships that start with the workers, that link to the community in which workers live, and have a larger than life vision around a social justice community that we're trying to build." Ross, Purcell, and countless others had joined SEIU in order to turn this vision into a reality.[54]

Labor at the Cross (Roads)

Fifteen years after John Sweeney assumed the presidency of the AFL-CIO on a platform emphasizing new organizing, and five years after SEIU president Andy Stern led a breakaway coalition from the AFL-CIO on the premise of bringing millions of new members into unions, the rate of private-sector union membership in the United States in 2010 was a meager 6.9 percent, the lowest rate since the early 1930s.[55] Among those scholars committed to union renewal, a vibrant debate has taken place about the relative merits of "top-down" versus "bottom-up" approaches to union expansion. Some scholars have emphasized the importance of union outsiders and centralized leadership to organizational reform and organizing success;[56] others have seen these same activities as undermining union democracy and rank-and-file leadership.[57]

These scholarly debates have taken on increasing significance in light of recent internecine labor struggles.[58] In the middle of the campaign at Santa Rosa Memorial Hospital, for example, the international SEIU union put the local union in trusteeship, effectively firing most of its staff (see chapter 5). Around the same time, SEIU became embroiled in a dispute with one of its longstanding allies, UNITE HERE (Union of Needletrades, Industrial and Textile Employees, Hotel Employees and Restaurant Employees), for which SEIU drew condemnation from virtually every corner of the labor movement.[59] Although many different accusations flew among the various sides in these fights, underneath the invective were real differences in the ways that these unions understood how to achieve power for workers and for the working class.

The campaign at Santa Rosa Memorial Hospital, and the broader strategy of organizing Catholic hospitals of which it was a part, blurs some of the distinctions between bottom-up and top-down unionism, while introducing new tensions and contradictions. The Memorial campaign relied on the commitment of a dedicated group of worker leaders, yet combined this grassroots commitment with top-down strategies such as national roundtable discussions among union leaders, bishops, and Catholic healthcare leaders (sponsored by the United States Conference of Catholic Bishops); alliances with Catholic scholars; and ongoing communication with system executives.

More generally, for cultural struggle to be effective, leaders must conduct intensive education and training among workers—both helping them appreciate a larger vision of unionism and working with them to become symbolic actors on a broader stage. But preparing workers for effective bottom-up participation is itself something of a top-down endeavor.[60] Cultural struggle must center on the experiences of workers themselves, but work on multiple levels—through insiders and outsiders, workers and intellectuals—to cast workers' interests as being in the common interest.[61]

But if the campaign at Santa Rosa Memorial Hospital helped to reconcile competing conceptions of union power, at least to some extent, reconciling these competing conceptions is insufficient to create an effective cultural strategy. A union debate that focuses on the best strategy to win power for workers misses the importance of *meaning* for these workers. And while increases in workers' control over wages and working conditions can be experienced as liberation,[62] the hospital context demonstrates the ways in which this control—narrowly conceived—neglects important dimensions of workers' emotional lives.

Discussing her vision for labor unions, one leader in the Memorial campaign contrasted her own position with those in the mainstream of the labor movement today. Many unions had "placed their hats on 'let's build power, political power, and then we'll take it forward from there.'" But for her the *ends* were as important as the *means*: "For me it was always about building a community predicated on love, power, and justice. So I want to build power, but I want that power to be linked to a vision of something that's greater than my self-interest." She was frustrated that union leaders would talk about how to "get more power" in a manner "delinked from justice and love." The irony, for her, was that her own vision of unionism was "very consistent with what these Sisters are trying to build. They're trying to build their kingdom of God on this earth." The labor movement, this leader implied, needed to be more self-reflective about the world it was hoping to achieve.

This vision is particularly well suited for an industry like healthcare, in which many workers are motivated by more than narrow self-interest, and in which corporations are particularly influenced by and enmeshed with cultural values. The task for the labor movement, then, is to develop what Antonio Gramsci calls a "concrete phantasy," a vision for the healthcare industry—and beyond—that connects workers' interests with the interests of all.[63]

An Outline of the Book

Throughout this book I suggest that labor scholarship has focused on how unions have been able to achieve economic power for their members without fully appreciating the implications of workers' emotional investment in their work or the ideological power of capital.

I first examine the history of Santa Rosa Memorial Hospital and workers' early attempts to organize a union with SEIU United Healthcare Workers West in 2004–05. Chapter 1 reviews the historical legacy of the Sisters of St. Joseph of Orange, and explores how the values on which the hospital was founded continue to find expression in the understandings and practices of workers in the hospital. The religious nature of the hospital is not only a historical legacy but also an important symbolic recognition of the social nature of hospital care, which infuses all work in the hospital, from the direct provision of care to the work that goes on far away from the bedside. This chapter also elaborates what happened as the Sisters gave up sole administrative control of the hospital, and the frustration workers experienced as the hospital administration instituted a more secular and more corporate regime—as it moved from the martyred heart to the managed, or *mismanaged*, heart.

In chapter 2 I recount workers' early organizing efforts in the hospital between 2004 and 2005, and the relationship between workers' desire for voice in the hospital and their emotional investment in their work. I demonstrate how the union campaign initially engaged workers' frustration over a lack of power more than it did workers' emotional commitment to hospital work. By engaging in a textbook antiunion campaign, the hospital was able to marginalize prounion worker leaders, intimidate union supporters, and undermine union strategy. As important, however, the hospital was able to frame the union as having interests that were opposed to the well-being of patients, the hospital, and the community. The divisive campaign was portrayed as being the fault of an external, "third party" union that would put the heart of the hospital—the direct care for patients—at risk.

At the end of chapter 2 I present the story of the union's political strategy as it moved from the workplace to the broader community. In so doing I diverge slightly from the chronology of the campaign, since the theological campaign (discussed in later chapters) began before and continued after this political campaign. Over the course of 2007, the union sought to intervene in a deal between a struggling local hospital and SRMH, in order to make the deal contingent on Memorial's willingness to negotiate "fair election" ground rules. This strategy was emblematic of the standard union "comprehensive campaign" or "corporate campaign," which uses economic and political leverage to win concessions from employers. This analysis helps to highlight what distinguished the ideological struggle from the strategies of more standard social movement unionism. The strategy was unsuccessful in its narrow political goals, but it *was* successful as one component of the broader ideological project.

I then examine the union's shift to a cultural strategy: from workers' positional power in the hospital to workers' relationship to the hospital's soul; from a focus on the workplace to a focus on the religious community and beyond. In chapter 3 I explain how SRMH fit into a larger "Catholic" strategy to organize Catholic hospitals within the national SEIU. That the union could wage a battle over the hospital's moral standing was made possible because of a unique cohort of leaders within the international SEIU; because of St. Joseph Health System's strong financial position, which made it unbeatable in the economic realm alone; and because of the clear contradictions between what the system asserted about its values and what it did in practice. In this chapter I also elaborate the terrain of the theological debate that would come to dominate the campaign—the theological arguments that the hospital and union came to make about the relationship between Catholic teaching and labor unions.

In chapter 4 I illustrate how the union successfully expanded the scope of conflict beyond the workplace, engaging broader religious and political communities in a campaign for a "fair election agreement" between

2005 and 2009. By building a coalition of Catholic religious leaders who became spokespeople for Catholic social teaching on the rights of workers, the union was able to challenge the St. Joseph Health System's monopoly on moral authority in the hospital. This chapter explores the creative ways the union built and made use of this coalition, and the tensions involved in these sorts of labor-community alliances. It also discusses how the role of workers changed as the campaign's focus shifted from workplace to altar.

At almost the very moment the union won its campaign for a "fair election" agreement, however, the international SEIU placed the UHW in trusteeship, firing its top staff and bringing the St. Joseph Health System campaign to an abrupt halt. Tensions had been brewing between the local and international for years, in part because of a personal clash between the local and international leader, in part because of real differences in how each conceived of union strategy. As workers at Santa Rosa Memorial Hospital reeled from the news, they began to regroup with a newly formed National Union of Healthcare Workers (NUHW) composed of a volunteer staff of former UHW employees. The staff dedicated to the hospital campaign dropped from five paid staff to one lone volunteer. SEIU sought to undermine the campaign to prevent NUHW from gaining a toehold at any hospital in California.

In chapter 5 I explore the internecine struggle between NUHW and SEIU as workers fought a third and final round for their union. Through this lens, I enter the contemporary debate on union democracy and union revitalization, particularly as it relates to the struggle at Santa Rosa Memorial Hospital. In this chapter I also explore how the trusteeship forced workers at Memorial to take ownership of the campaign in ways they had not been asked to before, and came together with almost no resources to take on a well-funded hospital system and a powerful union, who were now united in their opposition to the grassroots workers' drive to unionize hospital workers.

Finally, in the conclusion, I explore the implications of this study for the labor movement as a whole. I argue that while unions must continue to advocate for the material advancement of their members, they must see themselves less as interest-based organizations and more as *values*-based organizations. Unions must combine their instrumental focus on power with a narrative focus on meaning.

1

The Labor of Love

Vocational Commitments in the Hospital

Fred Ross and Eileen Purcell had known the Sisters of St. Joseph of Orange, the owners of the St. Joseph Health System, since the heyday of the United Farm Workers movement. In 1973, several of these sisters had gone to jail with striking farmworkers in Fresno. Since then, many had worked alongside Ross and Purcell for justice in El Salvador. In the late 1980s and early 1990s, the Sisters had supported the Justice for Janitors campaign in Los Angeles, and in 1995 one sister had founded Taller San Jose (St. Joseph's Workshop), a job-training program for at-risk youth in Santa Ana, California. It would have been more surprising had Ross and Purcell been able to *avoid* being familiar with these nuns, whose social justice legacy was well known across California.

An Introduction to the Sisters of St. Joseph of Orange

The Sisters of St. Joseph established themselves sometime between 1646 and 1651, when a Jesuit priest named Jean Pierre Medaille first arrived in

Le Puy, France, and helped to organize a lace-weaving cooperative among a small group of starving and war-ravaged women. As the legend goes, the women were able to support themselves on the proceeds of the trade, and dedicated their spare time to nursing the physical and spiritual needs of others.[1]

Whereas nuns traditionally had come from wealthy families and remained cloistered, or closed off from the outside world within convents, beginning in the seventeenth century a number of uncloistered communities were founded. In France alone, eighty such communities of nuns sprang to life between 1630 and 1720.[2] The Sisters of St. Joseph were one of these early groups of religious women, women who came from more modest backgrounds and who lived out their spirituality through works in the community.[3] Saint Vincent de Paul, one of the earliest proponents of this active ministry among religious women, is thought to have said to another uncloistered community, the Daughters of Charity, "When you leave your prayers for the bedside of a patient, you are leaving God for God. Looking after the sick is praying."[4]

The culture of the founders has remained remarkably resilient across time and place. For the Sisters of St. Joseph, one of the first orders made up of ordinary women, and one of the first to reject the cloistered life, spirituality is something brought to life in the sweat and toil of good works. As they arrived in the United States in the mid-nineteenth century along with other orders of Catholic women from France, Ireland, Great Britain, Germany, and Poland, these religious women represented "a hybrid form—pragmatic and worldly, vocation-driven and deeply religious at the same time."[5] Their successful institution-building and care for the poor made them the most visible ambassadors of the Catholic Church to an often-suspicious Protestant majority;[6] many of those Protestants most skeptical of Catholicism made an exception for these religious women.[7] Catholic Hospitals also gave nuns important sources of institutional and spiritual autonomy from the male-dominated Catholic Church, especially for those orders—like the Sisters of St. Joseph of Orange—that were structured around a central motherhouse rather than around a local diocese.[8]

In 1918, the Sisters of St. Joseph of Orange began caring for the sick and poor in the small community of Eureka, California. A delegation of sisters had been sent there from their headquarters in Orange, California, to found a school, but saw the local community being ravaged by the global influenza pandemic that ultimately killed 50–100 million people world-wide. In response, they began visiting people's houses, and eventually set up what would become St. Joseph's Hospital. But despite their efforts, the Sisters faced the skepticism of a recently professionalized medical community, who "were reluctant to bring their patients to St. Joseph's, for they believed the Sisters were untried and uneducated."[9] It was only through three years of arduous work and training that the "rooms were filled and . . . ledger books indicated that the convent would be enjoying some financial security."[10] Over the next several decades the hospital system grew—to four hospitals by 1933, and to nine by 1964; throughout this period the Sisters themselves held nearly all of the administrative and staffing positions in their facilities.

Just as the Sisters of St. Joseph of Orange established themselves in Eureka, sisters throughout the United States mixed selflessness and vocational devotion with business sense and political acumen. On the one hand, sisters found deep spiritual meaning in patients'· physical vulnerabilities, and fluidly mixed the care of patients with their own religious practice.[11] On the other hand, these same sisters transformed "overwhelming social need into opportunities for the development of health care services to the American public," and established themselves as among the earliest female entrepreneurs in the United States.[12] During the nineteenth and early twentieth centuries, women's decisions to join religious orders were often connected to considerations of economic power in a world of precluded possibilities.[13] Indeed, it was Sisters' religious identity, sexual chastity, and relative anonymity that allowed them the institutional space to build their own organizations within a broader patriarchal society,[14] freeing them up to act "like men" well before other women of their time.[15] For example, Sister Jane Frances Power, mother superior of the Sisters of St. Joseph of Orange beginning in the late 1960s, was the first female head of the Southern California Hospital Council beginning in 1964 and the first president of the St. Joseph Health System. Describing her, a former sister said, "Before I knew that there could be women who just manifested more masculine traits, and they still were women in every bit of themselves, I would have said 'She should have been a man.'"

Catholic hospitals exemplified the midcentury ideal of selfless voluntarism, an ideal that shaped hospital practice and policy nationwide. Catholic hospitals relied on the low-wage labor of the nuns.[16] But the idea of voluntarism in hospitals stretched beyond the Catholic hospital as well. In secular hospitals, auxiliaries—or unpaid volunteers—made up for what the organizations lacked in religious zeal. As late as 1961, there were 1.2 million members of such auxiliary organizations (most of them women), which was not far from the total number of paid employees. These volunteers, like the nuns in Catholic hospitals, brought to life the idea of the hospital as a local community institution, and the idea that hospital work was something done for more than economic motives.[17]

Even today, nuns continue to be free from the demands of husbands and children, · independent from obligations to the "private sphere." Their commitment to God seems to provide a kind of legitimacy to their femininity—a marriage to Christ.[18] And so, somewhat paradoxically, they remain in some ways less constrained by conceptions of femininity than other women are, and more free to engage in the public sphere whole-heartedly.[19] Because of their unique capacity to be both moral leaders and entrepreneurs, nuns remain influential players in a hospital industry that profits in part from being seen as something *more than just an industry*.[20] As one indicator of this influence, Sister Carol Keehan, president and chief executive officer of the Catholic Health Association (CHA), was named the most influential person in healthcare by the trade publication *Modern Healthcare* in 2007.

A potent mix of business and spirituality continues to infuse the way that Sisters and lay executives in the St. Joseph Health System explain the organization's day-to-day work. According to one system executive, "It's very easy to define your actions in terms of the environment and the market. . . . But we try not to ever approach a problem from the viewpoint of the market, but from the viewpoint of the ministry, operating within a certain market." A nun on the executive team explained how the system was always deliberate about "framing it" in such a way that the "finances are what supports [us] doing the ministry." She spoke of the administration's responsibility as "stewards," adding that "what we have to steward is way more than money. It's reputation and history, the people that are involved, all of the assets, the buildings, the facilities, the good name in the community."

What does it mean for the ministry to take precedence over the market within the operations of the hospital system? One executive explained: "We believe that the experience of interacting with us has an opportunity for a sacred encounter, sacred meaning. You walk away from the encounter more whole than you came into it, whether you [are] a vendor or an employee or a physician." Recognizing the challenge of institutionalizing the sacred encounter in a system with thirteen hospitals and over twenty thousand employees, the Sister emphasized the importance of spiritual "formation":

> We have been striving to give people the opportunity to reflect on what a "sacred encounter" is. That's formation. "When did you feel respected, healed, whole by an interaction with a person? When do you think you've been able to be an agent of that for someone else?" That's the kind of reflection.

Another executive acknowledged that this sacredness was hard to measure. Still, the system had been working to take "particular moments in the patient experience" and explore how to make them more sacred. For example, she explained, "One of the places we realize that there's a real opportunity for sacredness is around the birth of a child. So we're looking at that moment and saying, 'What do we do in that particular moment that enhances the opportunity that it be perceived as a sacred experience?'" The sacred encounter provided an orienting vision among the hospital leadership about what kind of environment they should be striving toward.

Sacred Encounters from the Bottom Up

When workers described what connected them to the hospital, very few addressed the religious nature of the work explicitly. But the idea of sacred encounters was echoed in their descriptions of those social dimensions of their work that they valued most—a connection to patients, to one another as they worked on behalf of patients, and to the kind of collective effervescence that arises when people rally together in times of uncertainty and crisis. The sacred encounter, as an ideal, seemed to resonate with workers' investments in the work they did.

Louise, a licensed vocational nurse and union leader, echoed the sentiment of some nuns when she discussed changes in nursing she had observed as nursing pay had increased: "People started going into nursing that really had no business doing it, they did it because the money looked good. And so they didn't have the calling to be a nurse." It "shows in the way they relate to patients." In explaining what was missing from those nurses who "didn't really want to do nursing," Louise described the personal, social, and psychological dimensions to nursing work that go beyond the daily requirements of the job. When a person has a trauma to his or her body, she went on, "there's a big mental thing you go through," fears of never feeling normal again. Yet "some people won't ask you those things . . . that's too embarrassing to ask you." It was only through "getting personal" that nurses were able to draw out and address these fears: "By giving somebody a bath and washing their hair, you're teaching them all the time you're doing that."

Workers at a hospital are surrounded by people coming to terms with their own limitations and, in some cases, their mortality. Although there is certainly variation in the ways that workers relate to this emotional intensity, many felt that it made the work more meaningful and more significant to their own lives than if this aspect of work had been absent. Louise explained how, in the hospital, "We take everything away from them. We tell them when to eat, when to sleep, when to get up and sit in a chair, when to walk around the halls. They don't really have a say." She suggested that this loss of control was especially hard for men, who are "used to being really independent." Rebecca, a unit secretary at the hospital, said that one of the facets of work she enjoyed most was "being involved with people in a very sort of intimate way. Just seeing them as no one else sees them and being able to know that I know them and that they know and trust me." Frank, an anesthesia technologist, felt the weight of the responsibility: "Somebody's gotta be their advocate because they're at their most vulnerable when you get them. They're trusting you with their lives. You're going to put them into unconsciousness and they're going to trust you to take care of them." George, a respiratory therapist, distinguished between the cerebral and the emotional aspects of his job:

> There's numbers, a person has a pulse, a person has a breath rate and a breath sound. But they also have a psycho-emotional part of them that's dealing with the vulnerable, compromised state that they're in. Whether it's having a hard time breathing, with asthma, or being in a trauma and being banged up and being on a breathing machine and being really afraid.

He described a patient who had been hit by a truck while leaving work one day and had been flown by helicopter to the hospital. While she could not write or speak, George remembered that "she was very much there, I could see that in her eyes," and saw that she was "distraught" and "frustrated." George knew of an underutilized valve that he could use to let someone speak even while on a breathing machine, and convinced the trauma surgeon to insert it. "And she was able to talk—you know, and express, 'This hurts, that hurts, I'm hungry, I'm this, can I have that, what's the next step?'" Combining his technical expertise with his emotional attunement, George was able to give this patient her agency back.

The emotional intensity of hospital work creates a particular kind of community among workers at the hospital. Mari, an obstetrician technician, remembered that "many times when we lose somebody we cry, we just hug each other, and we got to continue with it." Because of this intimacy, "it is a family, you become a family" with your co-workers. Yet workers' sense of the importance of their work was not necessarily related to their proximity to patients' vulnerability. Describing what she likes about her work, Cynthia, an imaging technician, said, "The service that we're administering is for the most part clear-cut about its needs; it's not like you're making a widget that no one really needs." Her skill was one that had a clear and immediate role in helping people get healthy, even though her direct interactions with patients were limited. José, a kitchen worker, had a similar feeling about what he did:

> What we do directly affects how the patient heals and gets better throughout their stay at the hospital. Doing day to day the work to get those meals ready, to get those plates clean for them, to be sanitized for them to be ready for the next meal, plays a big role in nourishing the patients. I may not have that contact but I think I play a part in it because we're all connected, you know, because if we don't provide them food we're not gonna heal them properly.

Even without personal, emotional connections with patients, workers in the hospital felt connected to something significant. Workers' feelings of emotional investment in their work meant that they were often willing to do more for their patients than required of them by their jobs. Louise explained how she went out of her way to make sure that dying patients had their needs met:

If they need to talk to everybody in their family and want to talk on the phone or whatever, you need to provide that for them, even if that means taking your damn cell phone and giving it to them. "Yeah, you can't make long-distance calls out of our hospital, here's my cell phone. Call everyone you need to call." Because you have to do what it takes.

More significantly for the hospital's bottom line, workers are often willing to work longer hours than those for which they are paid. Louise said that she'd rather "stay over and be late [getting] home" than let her patients be without something they needed. Rebecca admitted that she rarely took her break because her "main objective there is to make the patients get the best possible care." Frank remembered how he "gave [the hospital] a free hour every day for seventeen years to make sure that when the anesthesiologist got there there was nothing that they needed." This "free labor" is consistent with the voluntary ethos fostered by the hospital administration, but also seems structured into the nature of hospital work itself. Nurses are often cited by managers as exhibiting a reverse labor supply curve, in that the more they are paid the less they work, choosing to substitute leisure or family time for more hours on the job.[21] Although that doesn't hold up empirically,[22] workers' accounts at Memorial Hospital hint at an inverse curve of a different sort, as those people who feel so deeply connected to their work might be willing to put in *more* hours than those better compensated for whom the job is "only a job."

When the Sisters were an active presence at the hospital, they served as the example of a vocational commitment to hospital work. And while they had already begun to withdraw from daily work at the hospital by the time most current employees arrived, several workers recounted fondly the administrative roles that the Sisters continued to play. Louise remembered how the Sisters served as an emotional resource for patients: "I could always call them and say, you know, 'This person's having a really tough time, could you come over and just talk to them?'" But the support the Sisters provided Louise herself was just as important to her. Recalling how difficult it had been when she had patients pass away as a young nurse, Louise said, "They would seek me out in the lounge and ask me, 'Are you doing okay? Do you want to talk to me? I know you had a relationship with that patient, and how are you doing?'" Sisters' concern for their employees went beyond the workplace as well. Louise remembered how they asked her how her kids were and how she was doing as a single mother. Bettie, who works in Central Supplies, remembered that "people depended on them and they knew that they could go to them. They actually honestly listened to you and tried to help you."

While the Sisters were still actively administering the hospital, workers also felt that they had a means to discuss the difficulty of their jobs and come to collective solutions. One administrator, Sister Phyllis, would hold open meetings at which workers could talk about what was going on. Rebecca recalled how "people would be crying about how they wanted [more time] to care for the patients. And Sister Phyllis would follow up with everybody and try to see that the situation was rectified." These meetings would often stretch over several hours, giving space so that "everybody in the room who wanted to talk got to talk." Alexis called the Sisters "the conscience of the hospital," a buffer against financial concerns: "Whenever the hospital administration would start getting greedy and start thinking about money versus people, the Sisters would kind of go, 'Wait a minute, that's not how you treat people.'" Even as the Sisters' presence in the hospital diminished, Alexis seemed to think of them as guardian angels. Long after the Sisters had left active administration, there was a rumor going around the hospital that a Sister had played a part in getting a bad manager fired. This Sister, still involved in a local Catholic school, had seen the manager as a parent, "saw that her son was afraid of her," and then heard about her employees being unhappy. "I think [she] put two and two together and said, 'Yeah, this is somebody we don't want around here.'"

For several employees, the Sisters' religious conviction resonated with their own values even more directly. This was especially true among some Latinos at the hospital who were also practicing Catholics. Rosanna, a Latina medical translator, appreciated the chapel in the hospital and the visible presence of Catholic symbols and values. When her biological sister offered to help get her a better-compensated union position at a nearby facility, she declined. José also felt some resonance between the Catholic values of the hospital and his own values growing up: "Going to mass and church school, I mean, it really influenced me in the way I think and the way I carry myself." Soon after he began working at the hospital he realized that this work compelled him more than other kinds of service jobs he had worked before because of the way he was able to help out those in need, "nursing them with good food."

The Mission Meets the Market

Even those employees who remembered the good old days of the Sisters' involvement had arrived at the hospital during a period of flux in both the organization of healthcare and the organization of the Catholic Church. The passage of Medicare and Medicaid in 1965, and the large infusion of money into hospital care that followed, created a bountiful new environment for healthcare in the United States—an environment that was somewhat disorienting for the Sisters of St. Joseph of Orange. According to a history of the Sisters of St. Joseph of Orange, by the 1960s they were asking themselves, "Where did the vow of poverty fit into all of this material success?"[23] In 1967, the Sisters' monthly allowance jumped from approximately $30 (in 2005 dollars) to approximately $150. "It was the older Sisters . . . who had difficulty with this concept. They had never been asked to express any of these needs—how could they even imagine what they would use in the way of material goods?"[24] This relative opulence was accompanied by a loosening of other strictures. In response to Vatican II, in 1968 the Sisters retired the habit, were allowed to live in apartments away from the community, and were allowed to spend their leisure time more or less as they desired.[25]

But the opportunities within Catholic healthcare and the Catholic Church paled in comparison to new opportunities in the world at large. The social upheavals of the 1960s and 1970s far exceeded the new allowances of the order, and nuns began to exit in significant numbers. That decline has continued to this day. The written account records that during this era "a growing number of the positions [in the health system] were . . . being filled by lay persons."[26] Concerned that the hospital system not lose "Christ's healing ministry," yet not wanting to "impose their views on the increasingly diverse individuals that made up the bulk of their employees," the Sisters defined what values were most important to them as an order and then asked employees to define how they would live out these values. The Sisters' active presence in the hospital would decline, but they would still "retain full ownership of the hospitals, and also would select the . . . Board of Trustees, approve financial officers, and control the budget."[27]

Jill, a former nun with the Sisters of St. Joseph of Orange, remembered how exciting and uncertain a time it was for women in the order. While sisters were permitted to "shed the habit and wear street clothes,

I didn't want to do it," she recalls. And "when they went to Delano" to support striking farmworkers, she didn't go, "not because I didn't agree that the workers should be able to strike, [but because] I was afraid." The order's new engagement with the outside world also meant that it put a premium on Sisters' ongoing education, sending several to the East Coast for doctoral education in the 1960s and 1970s. According to Jill, the new academic opportunities for a few Sisters indirectly exposed all of them to new ideas:

> It meant that they were going to be with a lot of people who weren't in community and so learn other ideas, experience other things and so they came back and they brought a lot of that back to the community and they were actually the ones in the '60s that were pushing for change in community and change in the church.

These Sisters would bring modernity to the order, and represent the order in a modernizing world.

The Sisters' relationship with their hospitals began to change in some subtle ways as well. In the early years, with ready new cohorts of young recruits to staff the orders' hospitals and schools, the Sisters were able to support themselves in the cooperative manner of their founders. Sisters were given a nominal monthly salary, most of which went to a collective pot that would be used to pay for all Sisters' food, housing, and medical care. Yet where the Sisters who served as teachers were given approximately $60 a month when Jill worked, the Sisters in the hospital were given a salary equivalent to lay staff, which came out to be "a lot more." Therefore, while there were many more Sisters working in the schools than in the hospitals, all of the Sisters knew that "it's the hospitals that support you."

The division between teacher Sisters and hospital Sisters only deepened as the numbers of new recruits ebbed and the order came increasingly to rely on the profits from the hospital system to support itself. A new generation of Sisters in the hospital challenged the stereotype of the nun as an epitome of selfless femininity. Instead, those Sisters still involved in the hospital system were business-savvy executives. As a whole, Jill remembered, the Sisters involved in the hospital "didn't feel as sensitive, or as warm" as the Sisters involved in teaching. Moreover, the order would select the "more brilliant" Sisters from the ranks of the teachers and recruit them into the hospital system. Of those Sisters who received their doctorates, Jill remembered, many had been teachers before graduate school, but "not one of them went back to teaching." Paradoxically, it was the same spirit of engagement with the world that led the order both to its commitment to social justice and to its entrepreneurship in the hospital industry.

The steep decline in new recruits to the Sisters of St. Joseph of Orange, and to orders across the country, has continued with the same ferocity as the nation's acceleration in healthcare spending. According to a 2009 study by the Center for Applied Research in the Apostolate at Georgetown University, over 90 percent of U.S. sisters were sixty or older,[28] meaning that only a small percentage of sisters are now able to work. In Orange, California, a large retirement complex sits next to the Sisters' motherhouse for those Sisters now old and infirm. According to Purcell, the hospital system has become "not only a safety valve but also institutional parity. . . . It gives them standing in the institutional Catholic Church that has systematically disenfranchised them and taken no strides—until relatively recently—to protect them in their old age." The hospital system continues to provide both an important nest egg for retired Sisters and some degree of equality with men in the Church to whom they have so long been subordinate.

Changes in the organization of American medicine and the internal dynamics of religious orders put new sorts of pressures on all Catholic hospitals over the second half of the twentieth century. Barbra Mann Wall, a professor of nursing, describes these changes as "analogous to the crisp black and white colors of nuns' habits blending slowly into shades of gray."[29] New competitive pressures meant it was more difficult for Catholic hospitals to maintain their religious commitment to the poor and underserved.[30] Moreover, these pressures, combined with declining numbers of sisters nationwide, meant that administrative obligations were increasingly transferred into the hands of lay leadership,[31] and Catholic hospitals that were once run relatively autonomously were forced to consolidate into multistate, multibillion-dollar hospital systems. In 1981, the Sisters of St. Joseph of Orange integrated their hospitals under the umbrella of the St. Joseph Health System. These Sisters, along with Catholic healthcare institutions around the country, were being forced to reevaluate how religious values might be translated into modern healthcare practice.

Maintaining the Mission

In 2007 the last two Sisters at Santa Rosa Memorial Hospital left their posts to move north to Eureka, meaning that the hospital's relationship with the order attenuated even further. Still, the Sisters were not content to benefit financially from the hospital while allowing it to be transformed entirely into a business. For one union leader, the premium the Sisters placed on their legacy seemed closely related to the fragility of the order itself: "Legacy and memory become important to people who are dying. It's a funny thing. It's almost as if we think if we're remembered we will still live and if we're not remembered we'll die."

When I sat down with a medical administrator at the hospital, he told me about steps the Sisters had taken to preserve their legacy in the hospital's daily practice:

> And so now the Sisters have said to me and to my partners, my fellow administrators, "You're in charge. And we expect you to operate this hospital as we would, in keeping with the traditions of the Sisters of St. Joseph. We want you to go into the community, we want you to do good, we want you to take care of people who are unfunded and underfunded. We want you to improve the health of the community."

As a part of this process, St. Joseph Health System had paid for him and other administrators to "go on a pilgrimage" to Le Puy, to learn "about the founders and how awful life was in 1650." More concretely, a cadre of multidenominational chaplains continues to minister to the emotional and spiritual needs of patients, and the sanctuary at the hospital—with sun filtered through large stained glass windows—is so beautiful that a group of local Catholics has adopted it for daily mass.

St. Joseph Health System maintains in each of its facilities a department of mission integration, focused on ensuring the consistency of the Sisters' theology and hospital practice. A few years ago, the Sisters' first hospital in Eureka was in dire financial straits, but according to one executive it was "the only major provider in that area." As he perceived it, "Anyone else looking at the financial side of it would have exited the market because it just didn't make any sense." But SJHS "looked at the community, and we looked at who we are and we made a decision to stay in that market."

For an ethicist who works for the system, the fact that SJHS dedicates "a significant amount of money" to treat the uninsured was evidence of the ministry in action. He continued, "I'm sure there's not a CEO that wouldn't just love to have that money kind of available, as opposed to, on the other hand, they really understand why we do it, and it's not grudgingly that they do it."

Many workers at Santa Rosa Memorial Hospital were cognizant of the Sisters' good works within Sonoma County, where the hospital is located. Alexis remembered expressing worry that the hospital's community service program would decline as the Sisters withdrew from Santa Rosa and the hospital faced new budget constraints. In response to her concern, one Sister told her, "'Well, do you know of any other program [to close] that's been developed and supervised by the Sisters?'" Rebecca discussed the variety of community programs sponsored by St. Joseph Health System in the county each year, and how she was "astonished" at the amount of money they spent on "outreach programs, their dental program, all of this. Just a lot of money given to the poor and contributing to various things within the community.... And it's wonderful what they do." Yet she went on to describe the vacuum left by the Sisters as they withdrew from the administration of the hospital: "They've always been wonderful with regard for helping the poor. But they failed to see what was happening in their own house. They were all out in the community, [and] as this was deteriorating inside the hospital they didn't see it."

A medical administrator at the hospital put the point somewhat differently, speaking proudly of the hospital's two mobile clinics, its dental clinic, and its array of programs for the poor:

> There needs to be a profit or you can't take care of anyone, let alone people who are unfunded or underfunded. The ministry of the St. Joseph Health System is very clear about improving the quality of life and the community that we serve, and is very clear about taking care of all comers.

In order to engage in these charitable works, the hospital had to be "tops in our game," had to be "very frugal." Whereas in a different era the religious mission of the hospital was front and center, this administrator implied, the hospital's mission now required that the hospital succeed in the market. The mission and the market have become distinct from one another, with the hospital's market success making possible a *separate* religious mission to the poor.

Of course there is another way to see the new relationship between the mission and the market, in that the espoused mission of the hospital may itself contribute to its bottom line. As Pete, a union organizer, pointed out, patients "want to feel that they're more than just a number, [so] there's definitely a value to having a religious brand on your hospital." Its charitable works are also, in some ways, financially strategic. They assure the hospital's reputation, allow it to claim not-for-profit tax exemptions, and make possible a significant fund-raising operation that complements its medical reimbursements from government and private insurers. Mobile dental clinics and an urgent care center in an indigent community, moreover, help to minimize costly emergency room visits by the poor and uninsured—visits that are still almost as high in number at Memorial as at the smaller former county facility. Is the horse of the mission driving the cart of the market, or the other way around? It depends on whom you ask.

From the Martyred Heart to the Mismanaged Heart

Workers who have been at Santa Rosa Memorial Hospital for a decade or more have borne witness to changes affecting all of American medicine: new technologies, increasing government oversight, and new fiscal pressures to do more with less. All hospitals today must compete for the dollars that accompany patient utilization, and so all hospitals are compelled to engage in the same sorts of practices, including reducing the amount of charitable (free) care they provide, investing heavily in new technologies, increasing the provision of profitable services, negotiating more aggressively with insurance providers and physicians' groups, and using staff more "efficiently."[32]

Simultaneously, however, many of the technological changes in medicine have actually enhanced workers' capacity to care for their patients: new breathing machines have allowed respiratory therapists to help patients learn to breathe on their own; safer gasses and more sophisticated monitoring machines have allowed anesthesia technicians to feel more in control of patients' pain; increasingly integrated computer systems have decreased medical errors and increased workers' capacity to work together on behalf of patients. Other administrative and organizational changes may be disruptive but make intuitive sense, such as regulations that restrict employees' access to syringes and drugs; increasing oversight for regulatory agencies such as the Joint Commission on the Accreditation of Healthcare Organizations (JCAHO); and new attention to the patient's experience of and satisfaction with hospital care.

Yet while technological changes have in some ways made healthcare more effective, financial pressures have often eroded care in other ways. As a result of financial pressure to use hospital beds for only the most serious (and most lucrative) conditions, the patients who come to the hospital these days are sicker than they once were. Whereas a patient may have once come into the hospital with pneumonia and stayed for a week, Louise observed, patients today tend to "have multisystem problems." According to Rebecca, "because patients are sicker, you've got more order sets [for medications], more arrhythmias, more people coming in with weird things, you've got more sepsis, you've got more myocardial infarctions, and yet you're the person who remains doing your job." While George thanks new technology for helping him work in close coordination with his respiratory therapy patients, the same technology means that care is more time intensive and the "workload should adjust so that those things can be carried out." Alongside technological changes in medicine, the inpatient population has changed as well. Without changing staff arrangements, however, a sicker population means a slow but steady (and underrecognized) speedup among the staff of the hospital.

If anything, workers have felt the hospital move to *cut* staffing and reduce costs in ways that they feel sacrifice those vocational aspects of care they most enjoy. When Mari started working at Memorial as a nursing assistant in 1997 there were three assistants assigned for every twenty patients. Today, one nursing assistant must care for twenty patients on his or her own. Mari said,

> The bottom line is that the individuals who pay this price are the patients, because if a patient waits five minutes for us to answer the call light to see what the patient needs, it's one thing. But if you wait fifteen, twenty minutes, it is not acceptable, and it happens, more and more and more. You

know, if you want a glass of water you can wait ten minutes. But if you really want to go to the bathroom you can't wait. Or if you're choking . . . sometimes we don't know.

These sorts of cuts mean that workers struggle to keep up with the most pressing medical needs of their patients, and are unable to tend to their spiritual or emotional needs. Susan spoke about how she was unable to do the "smaller things" that she liked to do for people. "As far as comforting somebody," she said, she was often forced to rely on the hospital's small volunteer staff. And while "the volunteers are amazing," they just are not qualified to say things like "tell me about your cancer diagnosis now." Mari explained how "compassion gets lost" because people feel stressed: "It's more about liability now than [about how] the patient feels. You can cut corners anywhere as long as you make sure you don't become liable." As workers increasingly feel under pressure, they must cut out those aspects of care that are not measurable or medically justifiable. Louise lamented, "I'm an old nurse, I want everyone to have a bath in the morning, to get their teeth brushed, to get their hair brushed, to have fresh, cold water to drink before breakfast. And that's not a possibility anymore."

To add insult to injury, hospital management prohibits workers from discussing with patients what is going on with their other charges, meaning that they cannot tell their patients *why* they have been unable to meet their needs. Louise explained, "If I had a patient that was bleeding out and I had to hold their groin for twenty minutes, and then I went back into a patient's room, [managers] don't want you to tell them that you were busy doing something else." Mari discussed how this restriction estranges workers from their patients: "What do the patients see? The patients see your face. They do not see management . . . And they look at me as cruel. Because they're thinking, 'Where were you?' You're not going to tell them, 'I have 20 other people,' because you don't do that, you just don't do that."

Staffing shortages occasionally have led to more serious medical emergencies. As a respiratory therapist, George remembered getting called for a Code Blue on one side of the hospital, beginning to help a doctor insert a tube and manage the patient's breathing, only to be called for another Code Blue in the pediatrics ward. The pediatric patient was a complicated case, and the doctor was confused enough about the reading on the patient to begin to remove the tube that George had inserted. George had to "grab his

hand" to stop him, and help the child to the helipad, where he was trans-
ported to nearby Oakland's Children's Hospital. George discussed how
these kinds of incidents put his very professional identity at risk: "What if
those things would have happened concurrently and I wasn't able to give
attention to one or another, and there was a sentinel event and there wasn't
a respiratory therapist? Whose license would have been in jeopardy? Not
the hospital's. Moi." Rosanna, a medical interpreter, recalled a time when
she was the only interpreter on duty and had been on lunch break when
she saw a trauma helicopter landing. Having been scolded repeatedly for
not clocking out during lunches, she decided to continue eating in her car.
Upon return to the hospital the doctors in the Emergency Room were
looking for her frantically, unable to speak with the parents of a Latino
child who had been in an accident.

Staffing cuts have been accompanied by other sorts of changes that
erode the quality of care workers feel able to provide. Jorge, a laboratory technician and phlebotomist, was upset when managers came into
the hospital's laboratory to tell him "we want you to use the bigger
needles because they're cheaper"; bigger needles allow phlebotomists
to withdraw blood more quickly and "get to the next patient in line
quicker." He thought to himself, "Bigger needles? You're only looking
at a seventeen cents difference. At the end of the year you might save a
couple of bucks, but that's it." He continued, "You're going to make little
kids suffer [a] twenty, sixteen, eighteen gauge needle." The manager
explained that since thicker needles would draw blood more quickly,
there was less danger of blood clots, but Jorge felt that this medical justification for the change was dishonest. Frank discussed how managers
were pushing for quicker turnover times between surgeries, meaning
that workers were "cutting corners to do it." Patients sometimes noticed:
"I've had patients—I know this is bad—you lay them down on the bed
and they've got those overhead lights that they put on, and they go, 'Oh,
look at the blood on the light!' I don't know how many times I've seen
the [lights] hanging there just before the patient comes in and I've taken
them away because somebody missed what they were doing because they
were trying to move so fast."

At the same time management has pushed workers in ways that compromise the work in which workers are invested, it has paid new attention
to "customer satisfaction" measured by patient surveys. As a result, the

hospital has moved toward a regime of the "managed heart," or more accurately the "*mis*managed heart." Cynthia put the point succinctly: while administrators want workers to treat patients "like royalty as much as possible, the thing that is going to come into conflict with [that] is staffing, because I know that sometimes they're staffing really low on the floors with aides. That's a problem, because [aides are] mostly the people who would be the first responders to that kind of stuff." The combination of cutbacks, on the one hand, and focus on the patient as a "satisfied customer," on the other, has led managers to engage in the kind of emotional coaching that Arlie Hochschild observed in her study of airline attendants.[33] Betty was told that she did not smile enough. During one evaluation, after Rebecca had spoken with her supervisor about the level of stress she felt on her job, her supervisor suggested she create "stress-relieving goals" such as taking a vacation or getting a massage—ignoring the work-related causes of her stress. Susan learned to act as if she had time for patients even when she did not: "You can use your body language and make it feel like you have the time. . . . It's not easy to, it's a strain now." After taking away resources employees felt were necessary to care for patients, managers coached workers to *act* invested in work from which they were increasingly alienated.

Workers at Santa Rosa Memorial Hospital are steeped in the history and values of the Sisters of St. Joseph of Orange during orientations and yearly evaluations, but for hospital management these values seem nearly indistinguishable from values applicable to any type of service work. When I attended an orientation for new volunteers at the hospital, a video on the Sisters' history was followed immediately by a video entitled *The Simple Truths of Service* based on a book by the same name.[34] In the video, Johnny, a grocery bagger with Down Syndrome, starts putting handwritten "thoughts of the day" in customers' bags, inspiring customers to come back to stand in his line. When the video finished, the trainer turned to the volunteers and said, "We want you all to be Johnny." It seemed odd that a hospital, which must deal daily with patients' vulnerability and uncertainty, would show a video situated in a grocery store. Since the practice of medicine has now become as impersonal as the grocery store, the implicit message seemed to be that the personal touch must now be produced intentionally.

It is unclear whether the focus on customer service—or even thinking of patients as "customers" at all—is in the best interests of patients themselves. Workers discussed at length the steps the hospital had taken to give it the feel of a hotel. Most infamously, a former CEO decided to lay down expensive patterned carpet throughout the facility. "Now it's all torn up because you can't have carpet in a hospital," Betty said. "Blood and piss and stains." Others recalled how difficult it was to push beds across the carpeted floors. Eventually they replaced the carpet with equally expensive faux-wood laminate, which, Betty explained, was not much better: "First Center East had so much traffic within the first couple months that they started getting big bubbles in them. So they had to split them." Dan, a radiology technologist, spoke of how the beautiful new laminated floors had already been replaced twice, and assumed the hospital would "have to go back to a more sensible flooring."

Other examples of questionable expenditures abounded, from the expensive oak chairs in the cafeteria (nice for sitting, impossible to stack, and difficult for the Nutrition Service workers to move), to the elaborate sound-sensitive traffic lights (green, yellow, and red) that were installed in the hospital's hallways as part of an initiative to keep the hospital quiet and alert workers when they were being too loud. Betty explained, "Every time I have to take a cart over to that east side I dread it. Those carts going over the threshold from the link to the hallway into the elevator, boom, bang, you know, there's just no easy way to do it. They either need to come in and get all brand-name carts, or something [else], because I hate having to do that in the middle of the night." Many of the bathrooms in the facility have hand-set, half-inch tiles that line the walls. When I spent time in the facility, the administration had recently decided to stop calling "Code Blues" over the hospital's intercom, as one doctor explained, because patients do not like to think about death. This had led to some close calls among the medical staff, who were alerted to medical emergencies by beepers. Meanwhile, a treacly lullaby was broadcast over the intercom every time a baby was born—apparently because patients *do* feel happy at the thought of a newborn.

Workers expressed frustration at how decisions were made at the hospital as much as they did at any particular decision. Dan, a fifteen-year employee at the hospital, had seen four CEOs come and go, each of whom instituted new plans and policies without the involvement of workers, nurses, or even doctors. Louise noticed that "there's always something new" in the hospital, and that while the administration used to "bring [workers] into" discussions of changes, "now it's just, 'We had a committee we put together, we've decided you're going to do this now.'" She attributed some of this change to new demands on supervisors: "They have nine million meetings management requires them to go to, and so it's not their fault." On three or four occasions Rebecca had offered advice to management about making her unit run more smoothly, only to be met with silence. The most frustrating time for her was when management had put together a committee to improve patients' perceptions of the nursing staff. Rebecca had several ideas for improving these relationships, but was not acknowledged when she volunteered to serve on the committee. She soon realized that they "weren't trying to get people's opinions, [but rather] wanted to educate people" on the computerized evaluation system they had already decided to implement.

Increasingly, workers felt regarded as interchangeable parts. Frank discussed how stringent management had become about workers clocking in and out so as not to earn overtime. In a conversation with an anesthesiologist, the doctor said to Frank, "'They want you to be robots.'" Frank agreed: "That's exactly what they want. They want us to be robots. Just do what you're told, and do it when they tell you and don't think on your own. Don't take any initiative." This feeling was exacerbated when, in the early 1990s, the hospital sought to cross-train all service workers in doing the basics of patient care—something the hospital referred to as "patient-centered care." The hospital fired all of its phlebotomists, with the idea that it would teach most service workers to draw blood and administer EKGs (electrocardiograms). Allison, a unit secretary, recalled being "way outside my comfort zone. I had been a paperwork person since day one, and I never imagined myself as a people person, let alone taking care of sick people." Jorge remembered how two patients died as a result of amateur blood draws. In one instance, an employee had accidentally given the wrong blood to a trauma patient: "She was just crazy because she had thought she had killed this person. The person was dying at that point anyway. . . . But can you do that to a nineteen-year-old girl and then have her think that she had killed this person?" At that point the hospital reversed itself, rehiring specialized phlebotomists.

Workers' feelings of exclusion from decision making was aggravated by the sense that financial decisions were consistently made at their expense. Workers are the first to be asked to reduce their hours when there are fewer patients than usual. When the Sisters ran the hospital, workers were given annual Christmas bonuses. But in recent years hospital management had eliminated the bonuses, apparently using the same money to inspire frugality on the part of managers. A prevalent rumor among workers was that department managers who came in under budget were given half of the cost savings in bonuses. Jorge recalled: "We even had a phrase that we would kick out there during each quarter when [managers] get their bonuses: 'Let's see how many brand-new cars the supervisors and managers bring in on the days after.'" Frank thought that supervisors' personal incentive to cut costs was at least partially responsible for their persistent emphasis on coming in under budget: "It's cutting and lining their own pockets."

Several workers were dismissive of the hospital administration's attempts at regulating their emotional lives while, at the same time, they were committed to bringing "authentic" emotions to their patients. As Brandon, a lead SEIU organizer in the drive to unionize Santa Rosa Memorial Hospital, said, "Workers really believe in [the values espoused by the hospital], they really do, but they'll say all the time, 'We're the ones who make these values real, not management.'" To some extent, then, workers seem to understand their "real" caring as a form of resistance—an assertion of values that the hospital leadership no longer truly supports. Of course, this sort of caring is one of the reasons that patients return to the hospital. On its own, then, this "resistance" only reinforces workers' marginalization within the organization—the *misrecognized heart*.

Vacating the Vocation

In the mid-1990s, a small group of Sisters of St. Joseph of Orange approached Father Ray Decker, a retired priest, legal scholar, and friend of the order, with a request. The sisters were going to vote for a new mother superior, and one candidate had suggested that the order get out of the hospital business altogether. Could Father Decker write a white paper fleshing out the theological argument for abdication? The move would not have been unprecedented. The Sisters of St. Joseph of Carondelet, a sister order based in the Twin Cities in Minnesota, had sold their hospitals and then taken the proceeds and founded several free clinics.[35] According to one union leader, these nuns believed that in the modern healthcare environment they could best live out their vocation by serving the poor.

In his white paper, Father Decker wrote that the mission of the Sisters of St. Joseph of Orange was "seriously jeopardized when the Congregation becomes so intermeshed and intertwined with governmental, medical and insurance institutions that it is serving more these systems than persons. The institutional restrictions now operative in the medical community make it impossible to serve the deeper calling which is to be identified with the ministry of Jesus . . . [and] to respond to the truly deeper spiritual needs of people." This new institutional environment contrasted with the Sisters' early history, he argued, in that earlier they had been able to "respond to [the medical and educational needs of people] simply and without needless complications," as Jesus had "dealt immediately and directly with those who came to him for healing, solace, or compassion." Moreover, he suggested, being entangled with the present-day medical system meant that "the survival of those institutions take precedence over the personal charisms [spiritual powers such as for healing] of its members, and in many cases even crushes those charismatic gifts for the sake of institutional survival." Father Decker concluded that the order should "divest itself of those institutions which are part and parcel of the present medical care delivery systems over which it has no control, and re-invest its financial and personnel resources in supporting the various unique charisms of its individual members." Father Decker's advice was not heeded, and the Sisters continued to serve as the owners of St. Joseph Health System.[36]

According to many workers, the values that the hospital publicly espouses have become little more than a patina of religiosity over an increasingly businesslike core. Frank said, with more than a hint of irony, "Everything's push, push, push as far as making sure you charge the patient, making sure you're not stockpiling, making sure that you've got the minimum you need for the time. They always are watching you and pushing you about that, and they call it '*being a good steward.*' There's no spiritualism in it at all. It's just sterile." José, a practicing Catholic, suggested the "values that they're preaching go to garbage" in management's daily practices. Dan assumed that the "suits are hiding behind these values. They're espousing them all the time and it strikes such a phony cord."

In the hospital's annual employee evaluations, workers are asked to discuss the ways they and their co-workers have lived out the values of the hospital. Interestingly, while the values publicly espoused by the hospital are "Dignity, Excellence, Service, and Justice," justice is excluded from the list in these evaluations. Moreover, each of the other values is interpreted in ways that are consistent with managerial priorities:

Adaptability—Service

- Seeks to understand and responds to changing individual or team priorities.
- Accepts and deals with changes positively.
- Accepts direction willingly in order to adapt his/her role to organization or team change.
- Supports team and organizational leaders in change implementation.

Communication—Dignity

- Smiles and greets others. Communicates in a respectful manner.
- Listens attentively to others to understand what is being said.
- Initiatives difficult or uncomfortable conversations including requests for personal feedback.
- Discusses private matters in a private area.

Continuous Improvement—Excellence

- Champions/supports efforts that boost the organization's overall efficiency and quality.
- Seeks help in understanding and incorporating SJHS best practices and continuous improvement philosophy.
- Uses experience, knowledge, and data to make informed decisions.
- Adapts to changing needs by acquiring new skills, knowledge, and behaviors.

Customer/Patient Focus—Service

- Attends to individuals needing assistance by saying "I will help you find out," rather than "I don't know" or "That's not my job."
- Seeks to understand and exceed customers' service expectations by creating an environment characterized by hospitality, trust, and a spirit of community.
- Makes response to patients and others served a priority.
- Seeks to provide assistance that respects cultural health beliefs and practices.

Supervisors then rank employees on a scale from one (below expectations) to four (exceeds expectations) in relation to these values. Several employees discussed the ways that the process seemed designed to discourage them. Dan referred to the evaluations as "intellectual purgatory," and suggested that his manager deliberately gave people low marks. If "everything's going smoothly," he observed, workers get a two out of four, "and you got to walk on water to get a four, so nobody generally gets fours." Since the evaluations are not tied to worker pay, Dan continued, "You'd think this would be used as a morale-building exercise." Instead, it seems, the evaluations were used in this department as a sort of annual repentance, a way for supervisors to demonstrate how workers might live out the hospital's values more observantly. Rosanna once overheard an administrator speaking with her supervisor about not giving high evaluations to employees because it might lead employees to ask for raises. A charge nurse admitted: "The joke is that you never hear of anything you do good, ever. And that is true."

At the same time, the small and symbolic ways that the hospital had once reinforced its values in daily practice were gradually eliminated. The hospital got rid of the Hawaiian vacation they once had given workers who had been at the hospital for fifteen years. The annual Christmas party was cancelled, as was the summer picnic barbecue. Workers were no longer given gift certificates to buy turkeys at Thanksgiving. Employees used to get a crate of oranges for St. Joseph's Day, but now they get bookmarks. Where workers were once given free meals on their birthdays, they are no longer given anything. The content of these perks were less important than their symbolic value as expressions of the Sisters' care for workers. Martha, a medical transcriptionist who had worked at the hospital for eighteen years, was laid off in 2007 after the hospital outsourced its transcription to a company in Colorado. Although she was disappointed at being forced to leave, it was the silence accompanying her departure that got under her skin. She worked from home, so her years at Memorial ended with a mouse click.

Workers were frustrated that the structure of work made the practice of the hospital's values impossible. Frank felt compelled to take a position elsewhere after working at Memorial for many years:

> It gets to the point where, you know, you just don't want to do less anymore.
> You don't want to compromise your patients anymore. You've been at this

home for seventeen years, and you gotta say good-bye. Because in your heart you can't tolerate that. And you won't be part of it. So you leave. You have no other recourse. If you [stay], you're less of a person, you have no integrity. You have to leave because it's just not tolerable anymore. I can't accept any less, that's not why I got into this business to take care of people. You don't compromise that.

Many workers have stories of co-workers, supervisors, or doctors who got fed up with the hospital. Alexis recounted how the head of the physical therapy department had resigned after the administration forced him to lay off his best supervisors. Jorge recalled how doctors were leaving Memorial for the other area hospitals. George remembered how, in the face of short staffing, "a lot of people left because they didn't want to work in that kind of environment."

2

LOSING IT

The Limits of Economic Interests and Political Power

Jorge is a middle-aged Latino, tall and broad-shouldered, balding on top with a ponytail that stretches halfway down his back. From afar he looks a little intimidating, but his easy smile and childlike laugh belie his tough façade. Jorge had initially trained as a psychiatric technician and found work at a local mental health facility, but because of his size "there was only one thing they wanted me for, and that was takedowns." He grew sick of being a "manhandler," and transitioned to work in SRMH's neurology department as a nursing assistant. When a phlebotomist position opened up at SRMH in 1997, he jumped at it.

In the fall of 2003, nurses at Santa Rosa Memorial Hospital—who were represented by their own independent union—had recently negotiated a two-year contract with a 14 percent annual pay raise. Other workers at the hospital were accustomed to the nurses getting higher raises than they did, but the hospital had typically given the "non-contractuals" something. Not this year. After two or three weeks without hearing anything, Jorge began speaking with other workers in the hospital's lab, and ultimately approached the department's new director to request a meeting. The director refused at first but ultimately capitulated, and about twenty workers gathered around a room as the new director defended the decision not to give them raises. The director first argued that too much money was spent on the nurses, and that the hospital was in tough financial shape. When Jorge replied that the hospital had publicly boasted of its recent record-breaking earnings, the tone of the meeting changed: "He got pissed off at me. And [he said], 'You aren't going to see any part of this. The reason the RNs got it was because they're more educated than you and you guys are no more than a dime a dozen. We can replace you just as fast as we lose you. And if you don't like that you can hit the road.'"

By this point Jorge's own blood was boiling. "I'm the one that brings in all the people that like to come here," he told the director. "We the people here in this room are the ones that have left the legacy, not people like yourself!" As the back and forth continued, the director finally provided an opening: "There's two reasons [the nurses] got the money that they got. One, they're RNs. Two, they had a contract." A light bulb went off. Jorge said, "That's all I need to know! It's over, it's done." And as the meeting wound down, Jorge's direct supervisor approached him and said, within earshot of the director, "Jorge, you're everything that he just said you were if you don't go in, right into my office right now and make that phone call." Jorge went into his supervisor's office: "I walked right into her room and I didn't know who to call! I didn't know what to do! But I knew I couldn't just back down." He walked back out into the hallway, grabbed the nearest telephone book, and started looking for a union to call.

Jorge wound up calling Glenn Goldstein, the organizing director of what was then SEIU Local 250.[1] Goldstein had been organizing in the healthcare industry for almost twenty-five years. He had been the founding organizer of District 1199NW (1199 Northwest) in Washington state,[2] and after coming to Local 250 in 1998 had directed Northern California organizing efforts during the successful Catholic Healthcare West campaign.[3] Glenn was also married to a critical care nurse, which gave him a deep personal understanding of the pressures facing healthcare workers. Glenn traveled to Santa Rosa from the Oakland headquarters the next day, and the organizing drive began soon afterward.

Exit, Voice, and Loyalty

This scene of direct confrontation between workers and managers over wages is reminiscent of union battles of old, and in some ways accurately reflects the history of Local 250, now SEIU-UHW. The union was founded in 1934 when nurses in San Francisco walked out as part of a general strike. According to several organizers, the union has had a long, militant history, in which workers and union leaders have been unafraid to do whatever it takes to win. Although the local had begun to change somewhat by the late 1990s and early 2000s, as it entered into more cooperative relationships with Kaiser-Permanente and CHW, most staffers and worker leaders in the local were still "more comfortable in head-on clashes," according to one union leader, than they were around a boardroom table.

In the fall of 2004, many workers at Santa Rosa Memorial Hospital—especially those service workers at the lower ends of the hospital's pay scale—were motivated to unionize by their own financial situation. One organizer involved in the campaign suggested that these workers "were getting paid way below the market level, compared to Kaiser, and it was an easy comparison to Kaiser," since Santa Rosa's Kaiser facility was only a few miles away.

Yet many workers approached the question of compensation ambiva-lently, which may help to explain their failure to mount a viable union campaign before the fall of 2004. Workers were unionized at both of the other two major hospitals in Santa Rosa, as were the nurses at Santa Rosa Memorial Hospital. All of these unions provided tangible evidence of what organizers call the "union difference." Frank recalled how the "nurses had a union, and it was like two different countries. You were either an RN, or you were a 'non-contractual.'" Mari knew the nurses and heard them talk about "'My contract, my contract, my contract.'" Moreover, Sonoma County was one of the most liberal counties in the country, represented en-tirely by Democrats in the state Assembly, state Senate, and U.S. Congress. If Catholic hospitals stand a chance of being unionized anywhere in the country, one would think it would be here.

In the sociologist Steve Lopez's insightful account of organizing efforts in and around Pittsburgh, Pennsylvania, he discusses how organizers had to overcome a legacy of business unionism and corruption in order to win the trust of workers.[4] Workers at Memorial confronted a different and more ambivalent legacy. Among these workers, it was not "do nothing" unionism but rather *militant* unionism that seemed to frighten them. As I stood with one political organizer at a sparsely attended rally in the fall of 2006, he contrasted the "middle class" workers at Santa Rosa Memorial Hospital with the "nursing care workers who are getting paid shit and really feel the need for the union." Another organizer referred to nursing homes as "the sweatshops of the healthcare industry." SRMH workers, the political organizer implied, did not feel the same urgency for representation that other workers did.

It was true that many Memorial workers tended not to be interested in the union if the union was understood as an adversary of the hospital. But this had less to do with workers being middle class than with workers' feelings of loyalty to the hospital as a community institution. Brandon discussed just how loyal most union supporters are to the hospital in which they work: "They might hate their boss but they will defend to the death the place that they work." As an organizer, he learned never to say, "This is a bad hospital." He continued: "Even at hospitals where workers will say things are really messed up and patients are at risk, they're still really proud of the work that they do and the work that their co-workers do. They clearly identify the boss as the problem." According to him, worker leaders at Memorial were actually those most invested in improving the facility: "The window through which I look into the healthcare workforce is the people who say, 'I want to work to make this place better,' and I think that kind of self-selects for a group of people who just generally care a lot more about what happens at the hospital than other folks might."

Interestingly, this meant that even a *positive* legacy of active unionism in other industries conveyed mixed meanings to hospital workers. Louise was encouraged to join the union campaign by her brother-in-law, who had worked for the Teamsters and "only said wonderful things about it." Despite this encouragement, Louise still had some reservations:

> [The Teamsters are] pretty radical for me, and as a nurse, coming from the place that I come from, you know, talking about walking out on my patients was like, I'd look at him and go, "What? What? I'm not walking out on my patients, are you crazy?" He said, "That's how you get things done." I said, "I can't hurt somebody else. I couldn't abandon them."

Susan thought initially that the union was going to "ask for more." She was not so supportive, since "I always felt like, you know, I'm not greedy." Dan was also wary about being part of too militant an organization: "I didn't enter this with any axe to grind. There's not a 'stick it to the man' kind of feel to it." Dan asserted that those who wanted the union didn't "want to kill the hospital. We want to be a thriving enterprise, we really do. Because a lot of people have been there a lot of years and have a lot invested."

Most workers who became involved in the union effort seemed to feel that the union would help them reclaim values that were central to their work—that the union would serve as a mechanism for voice. Albert Hirschman famously wrote of "exit" and "voice" as two mechanisms by which members of an organization can respond to its decline. Members can either leave, voting with their feet, or engage with the organization in an attempt to make it better.[5] In Hirschman's analysis, a key variable for understanding whether people will use exit or voice is people's degree of loyalty to that organization. The more loyal they are, the more they will have a propensity to use voice as opposed to exit. This framework helps us understand workers' desire for voice as a corollary to their feelings of loyalty to the hospital. And previous research *has* suggested that unionization increases workers' propensity to use voice as opposed to exit.[6]

Dan, a well-paid radiology technologist, said, "Interestingly enough, when you talk to employees, even though our wages are considerably lower than Kaiser, wages are not the main issue by a long shot." Rather, he continued, the idea that united workers more strongly was that of "voice" for themselves and their patients. Mari discussed at length the relationship between her feelings of loyalty to the hospital and her desire to make things better through the union. Working at the hospital, she said, "you become attached to your co-workers, they're your family." Even when offered a better paying job with fewer responsibilities at another local hospital, Mari said, she "did not want to leave Memorial because I don't believe that you can leave a place just for a better place. You don't abandon your house just because the roof collapsed. You build it better." She felt it would be "selfish" to leave: "Everybody in there is my community. I live here! All the people that work there are my friends, the people that are my patients, they're people that I interact with. So I wanted to put my little help in there to make that place better instead of abandoning [it] and going where the butter was."

A similar sentiment pervades the interviews I conducted with worker leaders of the organizing effort. According to Rebecca, those who were organizing "don't want to destroy, they want to make things better, they want to make their jobs run smoothly, they want it to run smoother for everyone else, they want the relationships between the nurses and other people in their work groups to be good." Louise discussed how all of the leaders of the organizing effort, herself included, "want to make our hospital a better place to give care and receive care, and we all want to be proud of what we do again." Louise was drawn to SEIU-UHW at least in part because it had established patient care committees at the hospitals it had organized. When she spoke with unionized workers at the local Kaiser facility, they reinforced the idea that employees "work things out about the patients with the management and with the nurses." According to Dan, a union would help people "be more emotionally invested in the institution, and they would work better for the betterment [of the hospital] if they felt their input was respected. . . . You gotta listen to the people who are actually on the ground doing the job." George echoed this sentiment: "I think you stifle creativity when you control, I think you open up those doors when you share ideas at a table for the betterment of the patient. . . . These big guys wouldn't be there without this whole army of staff who does a good job." Worker leaders seemed confident that a union would allow them to live out the values that had attracted them to medical work.

A union leader pointed out that "a lot of employers will look to the market to stay competitive and keep the union out" by raising wages to the same levels as those in unionized facilities.[7] But this strategy overlooked workers' investment in having a say over their work. And hospital leaders did not seem open to the idea that workers might make valuable contributions if they were included in decision-making structures. At one point during the campaign at Santa Rosa Memorial Hospital, for example, administrators put a cardboard cutout of the CEO in the cafeteria along with a suggestion box as a way of soliciting worker input. Some workers took pictures of themselves next to the cutout to poke fun at this sort of superficial attempt at inclusion.

Multiple Voices

Within the unionization drive, the concept of "voice" also helped to unify a rather disparate group of hospital workers in ways that a narrower, more material focus might not have. Workers in the hospital exemplify the extensive class differentiation within modern society: professionals and managers work alongside pink-collar nurses, white-collar bureaucrats, and service workers. Charitable and professional tropes have the potential of dividing workers from one another. Some workers making the same wages might see themselves differently because of their different proximity to patients (kitchen workers versus nursing assistants, for example), while some workers with the same proximity to patients might see themselves differently because of different salaries and different relationships to professional associations (nursing assistants versus anesthesia technicians, for example). The bargaining units at Santa Rosa Memorial Hospital that organized with UHW included nursing assistants, whose mean annual income in California was $27,450 in 2009, and nuclear medicine technologists, whose mean annual income was $86,590.[8]

Brandon suggested that two overlapping groups were typically most interested in organizing: "The people who do the most patient care, and the workers who are the most marginalized." These two groups are not mutually exclusive, he continued, but are more like "a Venn diagram." Workers such as nursing assistants, laboratory assistants, and phlebotomists are both directly involved in patient care *and* "on the low end of the totem pole in the hospital hierarchy." Workers such as dietary workers and housekeepers are marginalized without being in close contact with patients; and workers such as respiratory therapists, surgery technicians, and imaging technicians are involved in patient care and are relatively well compensated.

Pete, a union organizer involved in the Santa Rosa campaign, complicated this analysis in two ways. First, he suggested that there was a *status* hierarchy among hospital workers that mirrored pay differences, meaning that professional workers were more likely than others to be considered "leaders" by the workforce as a whole. In other words, although they made up a smaller *percentage* of the workforce than lower-paid workers, organizers needed to target professionals given their influence among the workforce as a whole. Second, he continued, professionals were more likely to be in favor of unionization for vocational (as opposed to financial) reasons. Whereas low-wage workers "are always going to look at the union as a protection, as an insurance, as a way to guarantee wage increases," professionals were more likely to think about the ways that unionization might allow them to be better professionals.

Existing scholarship supports the idea that healthcare workers support unionization for a variety of economic and vocational reasons.[9] Indeed, throughout the nonprofit sector, according to consultants Jeanne Peters and Jan Masaoka, "unionization appears to stem not only from [workers'] desire for better salaries but also from their unmet expectations about the distinction of their work culture from corporate or bureaucratic culture."[10] Among professional employees, support for and involvement in unionization efforts appears to be driven by a desire for professional growth and patient care more than by traditional wage and benefit concerns.[11] Consistent with this idea, the financial benefits of unionization among hospital workers seem to be higher for low-income workers than for professionals.[12]

It seems safe to assume, then, that among the different groups of employees at a hospital there will be quite different motivations underlying the desire for unionization. Some have argued that in this context a craft-union approach, by which a union organizes a particular occupational group across different workplaces, might be more successful than an industrial approach, by which a union organizes all workers in a particular workplace or industry.[13] Nurses in California, through the California Nurses Association (CNA),[14] have certainly had tremendous success as a craft union. But other than the nurses, who together made up approximately 28 percent of all hospital employees in 2008,[15] most occupational groups in the hospital make up much smaller percentages of the workforce, meaning that their leverage as separate occupational groups would likely be quite small. Moreover, separate occupational unions would run the risk of competing with one another over wages, benefits, and voice over the organization of work. And while a craft approach may unite those workers with the most similar interests, there is reason to suspect that craft unions actually undermine the organization of less-skilled workers. In their compelling historical study, the sociologists Michael Hannan and John Freeman show that the density of craft unions had a negative impact on the survival of industrial unions, particularly in environments in which industrial unions were not common.[16]

The debate over the relative merits of craft and industrial unionism has persisted in different forms over the last century—between the Knights of Labor and the American Federation of Labor (AFL) in the late nineteenth century; between the AFL and the Industrial Workers of the World (IWW) in the first decades of the twentieth century; and between the AFL and the Congress of Industrial Organizations in the 1930s and 1940s.[17] Most organizers within UHW seemed to come down firmly on the side of industrial unionism, committed to organizing workers as *workers* and to breaking down occupational boundaries that might otherwise have separated them. The challenge for the union, then, was to "manage this tension" between workers' different motivations, and to make the case that these diverse groups of workers were better off standing together than standing alone. For Brandon, this was part of what he had "come to love about hospital organizing," given that "you really are organizing across race, across income levels, across gender, language, and everything." But he admitted that some technical workers would say things like, "Why can't we just have a union for the radiology technicians, we don't want the housekeepers." Pete discussed how some technical workers "associate the word 'union' with the old industrial unions, autoworkers, farmworkers." He continued, "Some respiratory therapists [say], 'Why do I want to be in a union with housekeepers? Why are you sticking me with them? I'm a professional.' There's a lot of that in hospitals and healthcare. It's very hierarchical." Nevertheless, Brandon discussed how workers of many different stripes often came to see their common interests fairly quickly:

> You overcome it by having an organizing committee that has people from all those different areas, and it's frankly surprising to me when I think about it how quickly people see that they at least have a common interest. Because whatever the political issues are, everyone wants more of a voice, they want more control over the work that they do. I think that's one of the realities of working in this capitalist economy. People have so little power over the eight hours a day that they spend at work and everyone wants more power and they should have it.

Brandon suggested that "voice" and "power" are nearly synonymous, and that *all* workers want more of both. He assured "folks with more formal education" such as the respiratory therapists that they would make the decisions on behalf of their own department: "Just like you guys wouldn't tell the housekeepers how to clean the floor because they know how to do that better than you, they're not going to tell you how to ventilate a patient because you know how to do that better than they do." And he warned them, "You're not going to be able to address your issues if it's just you guys, 'cause guess what? There's just twenty of you, and there's sixty housekeepers in this hospital, so do the math. The twenty respiratory therapists could have a union and not win anything, [and] they probably couldn't win a union to begin with." It is only with collective power, he argued, that winning voice is possible.

The idea that a union enhances workers' voice is not entirely intuitive. For example, union contracts often are designed to overcome the arbitrariness of management through standardized rules and procedures, without leaving much room for discretion on either side of the labor-management relationship. Explaining why she supported the union, Betty recalled how she recently had asked her director about hospital policy and had been told, "It depends on what your supervisor says." Betty continued, "The rules are not the same throughout the whole hospital. Rules are rules, they should be for everybody." Similarly, Frank described a desire to have "something written in a contract saying, 'This is what I do for x amount of money.' And if they deviated from that box I could say, 'Hey, you can't do that, I can't do that now.'" Although a contract might increase the predictability and fairness of people's everyday work, there are ways in which it might actually reduce the amount of discretion that both managers *and* workers have in changing the way work is done. Labor leaders are quick to point out that the details of a labor contract are all the result of negotiations, and that there is nothing inherently rigid or inflexible about it. Nevertheless, in practice, "power" and "voice" may not always be as closely linked as Brandon and workers themselves suggest.

The concept of "voice" was also used to frame some of the more material demands by workers. Claims to higher wages and more extensive benefits were framed as being consistent with a desire for reciprocity and for being heard. For Betty these issues elided almost seamlessly: "I always just felt that we should have some rights to be able to voice our opinion and have a say-so in some of these changes and what's going on as far as wages and retirement." Brandon also seemed to see wages as a symbol of respect when he spoke about the interests of housekeepers and dietary staff being "more often around wages, benefits, respect." Louise thought retirees should be offered the opportunity to stay within the hospital's health insurance policy: "When [workers] put in x amount of time for you, made sure that your hospital was built up, got your reputation up and running, and made that commitment to you, I think [offering a retiree insurance plan] is fair." Interestingly, Louise contrasted this desire for retiree health insurance with a rumor from an antiunion employee:

> One of the people that was against unions said to me, "Oh, it's just that these housekeepers want to make $35 an hour." And I said, "Where the hell did you get that from?" and she said, "Well, I heard them talking," and I said, "Well, you know what? I think you might have heard what you wanted to hear because anybody who has absolutely no education is never going to think they're going to make $35 an hour."

Although low wages were seen by hospital administrators (and even some workers themselves) as an indication of the vocational nature of this work, those who supported the union seemed subtly to have shifted the meaning of certain deprivations, conceiving of them as a *betrayal* of the hospital's values. Health insurance upon retirement would be "righteous" of the hospital. Giving housekeepers $35 an hour, absurd.

Round One

The first time I walked into the small organizing office at SEIU-UHW headquarters in Oakland, I was struck by two things. First, the place looked like an empty bomb shelter. Despite the priority that the union gave to organizing, the organizing office was windowless and spare. I would come to appreciate that this was because organizers were always out and about, working twelve-hour days in and around the hospitals they were organizing. The second thing I noticed was a picture of a network diagram on the wall, an elaborate snowflake, with workers' names linked to each other by lines—enough to make a sociologist weep with joy. Brandon was proud of this drawing. He and Joe, another organizer, had managed to establish relationships with a huge number of Memorial workers in a matter of a few months.

Something that made the Memorial campaign unique, Brandon recalled, was "how easy" it was to generate support for the union initially: "We had one meeting with five people and just about every subsequent meeting we had came from those five people or from other existing contacts, and it was all through word of mouth, all underground." Brandon and Joe would ask workers whether they knew of anyone else to speak with, and almost everyone would give them new leads. Brandon compared the hospital to "a little city," with "family connections and a lot of relationship connections." People tended to know one another, and in ways that were not immediately apparent. Brandon continued, "I just found out about this a while ago that there's a couple different groups of people that go bowling together at the hospital. They're in a bowling league. I've been working at this place for five years, I had no idea." In many cases, relatives set one another up with work at the hospital. Two of the earliest supporters of the union, Rebecca and Ron, were husband and wife. They and their son Tony all worked as telemetry technicians at the hospital. In other cases, workers had formed relationships on the job. And these relationships often transcended different departments, since certain positions in the hospital demanded that employees work throughout the facility. For example, Bettie, who worked in central supplies, discussed how she was "out and about all night, and I'm throughout that whole hospital all night long," so she could talk with "everybody." Brandon explained, "There's a high level of interaction between all the different [departments], because everyone comes to the cafeteria so everyone knows the dietary workers, the housekeepers are on every floor, nursing assistants are on every floor, everyone interacts with everyone else." Brandon also noticed that in general the hardest departments to organize were "groups of workers like pharmacy techs and medical records, because they're isolated and they spend so much time with their managers."

In Santa Rosa, the organizing campaign took off like wildfire. It was what organizers call a "hot shop." Within five or six weeks after going public in October 2004, 68 percent of the twelve hundred eligible employees in a combined service and technical workers' bargaining unit had signed a petition for a union election. Jorge explained that support for the union was rising, "numbers [were] popping up," and how the organizing committee "started going by what the books said." Brandon also described this stage of the campaign as being done somewhat by rote:

If you don't have a public majority it's going to be really hard to win this, there are some things that it's just how it works. If you're teaching someone how to drive, if the car doesn't have gas in it, you might really not want to put gas in your car but the car's not going to go anywhere. It's sort of the same thing with an election. You might really want everyone to stay underground, but you're not going to win if you do that. If people want to win, this is what they have to do; there's no democratic consensus to build around that.

The initial drive for the union was deceptively simple. The union filed its petition in December 2004, and a vote was scheduled by the National Labor Relations Board for early February 2005.

The hospital's management was relatively quiet until after the holidays. When managers did speak up, however, they spoke loudly and clearly. The hospital hired an antiunion law firm in order to turn opinion against the union, and ran a textbook antiunion campaign. On several occasions, union supporters were approached by their immediate supervisors. A nuclear medicine technologist was one of these workers: "[My supervisor] said, 'I'm disappointed in you for supporting the union.' He made it seem as if [union supporters] had somehow hurt him by supporting the union—he made it very personal."[18] A dietary aide recalled that workers in her department were brought together several times a week for "updates about the union," during which time supervisors would distribute antiunion flyers. A supervisor told a patient transporter in the Imaging Department, "The union is not a good thing. Anybody who wants the union in here is an idiot." A manager summoned Jorge to his office and questioned him about his union activity for over two hours. Mari recalled the manager of the Pathology Department telling her that she was not permitted to wear her union button. Another worker put up prounion flyers in her break room only to have them removed by the next day. This worker said, "It was easier to be against the union than to be for it. We were afraid to step out in support of the union." Two workers reported feeling that their union activity was putting their jobs at risk.[19]

Supervisors also told workers that a union might jeopardize patient care. One manager told a respiratory therapist about an incident in which a therapist at a different facility had been forced to go on strike while intubating a patient, putting the patient's life in jeopardy.[20] Another manager told a unit secretary that any wage increase would have to be accompanied by cutbacks elsewhere, "probably patient care or they'll have to cut your hours." A management flyer read that "SEIU organizers have routinely ignored Hospital rules and improperly gone into units, departments and even treatment rooms to campaign."[21]

Management's antiunion stick was accompanied by a carrot. Several years before, during an unsuccessful union drive by the Teamsters union at the same hospital, Jorge was approached by his manager and told: "You look like you're one of the people that people respect. So if you lighten up on [the union], we'll show our appreciation. You're making how much, $12.50 an hour? $13.50 from this point on." During the SEIU union drive, the message was similar if more subtle. Several employees were given unprecedented wage increases in the last two weeks before the election, or even offered supervisory positions within the hospital. During the fall of 2004 and the beginning of the new year, administrators actively sought out the advice of employees, asking them "what their 'issues' were," "if there was anything they needed," or if anything "could be improved."[22]

The administration articulated its message about SEIU most fully during a series of antiunion meetings in late January, during which managers showed workers carefully crafted PowerPoint presentations that made the case against the union.[23] Forming a union meant that workers would abdicate their authority to a self-interested bureaucracy, the PowerPoint presentations suggested. A slide with the title, "Does a Local 250 Contract Really Give You a Real 'Voice'?"[24] read, "SEIU Local 250 is a large, bureaucratic organization. All important decisions are made by the SEIU leadership." Rather than giving all workers a voice, the slide continued,

> In reality, only a few strong [union] supporters may be rewarded by the union with a seat at the bargaining table for having "delivered" a large group of new dues-paying members. Your right to continue to work directly with management to find common-sense solutions to problems may be severely restricted.

Union leaders were painted as power-hungry upstarts bent on profiting themselves: "Who would this small group of employees be? Would they represent your interests? Do you trust these individuals to decide your future?" The slides also suggested that workers would be taken advantage of financially. One slide informed employees that Memorial workers as a whole would be paying over $600,000 a year to the union, while another told workers that a union would not guarantee "any changes in work rules" or "any increase in pay or improvement in benefits." Indeed, workers could end up with far less: "Bargaining is a 'give and take' process. SEIU could trade valuable benefits you have now for things the SEIU wants."

Although unions were once necessary, the hospital's slideshow propounded, the National Labor Relations Act of 1935 (which, ironically, actually gave workers collective bargaining rights) had changed all that. According to the slides, "laws were passed to protect workers," and employers "realized they had to compete for good workers by consistently improving pay and benefits; offering opportunities for growth and advancement; [and] providing fair and respectful treatment." These factors explained why so few workers were currently members of unions.

In its last presentation before the scheduled vote, management used the specter of the strike to raise questions about the union's motivations. A slide with the heading, "SEIU's Slogan, 'We Are Striking to Improve Patient Care,'" suggested that SEIU did not actually care about the hospital's patients:

- SEIU *always* claims strikes are to improve patient care.
- This is an insult to every caregiver.
- Innocent patients and their families are the only ones who truly suffer the consequences of a hospital strike.
  As a result, any healthcare strike is hard to justify.

Another slide read, "Everyone (except the union leadership) loses in a strike. Employees who strike lose. The Hospital loses. The patients, their families and our entire community lose." Moreover, a strike would not work, since "the hospital can hire replacements for employees who strike. [Memorial] can even bring in qualified employees from other Saint Joseph Health System locations to work." The presentation implied that the union would not have to suffer the consequences of a failed strike: "If the strike does not work, the union can just walk away and try to forget it happened. The employees must try to pick up the pieces. It can take months or even years for the damage to heal." In sum, "SEIU does not operate hospitals, does not take care of patients and has no long-term stake in the success of [Memorial]." Moreover, another slide declared, "there are few, if any, unions who call strikes as frequently and irresponsibly as SEIU."

The strategies used by hospital management are all standard fare among antiunion employers, and the labor scholars Kate Bronfenbrenner and Tom Juravich have demonstrated just how effective these sorts of tactics can be.[25] In their study, unions won approximately 85 percent of certification elections in the public sector, yet only 48 percent in the private sector. The authors demonstrated that employer opposition explained much of the variation. Employers that used many antiunion tactics in concert, as Memorial did, were able to limit union victories to less than 40 percent.

Several employees recalled management's antiunion practices as having a chilling effect. George discussed the fear that arose for him when he began to get involved in the union: "Am I going to put my job in jeopardy? Hell, yeah." The day after his picture appeared on a union flyer his director came to observe him work, something rare for this supervisor, and seemed quick to notice flaws in George's work: "'How come this patient's head of the bed isn't at 30 degrees?' 'Well, because that's a rotating bed, it can't go 30 degrees.' 'Why's that patient almost out of pain medication?' 'Well, the nurse is trying to get that patient's pain under control.'" The director then took George aside and said, "Is there something that I've done that's caused you to seek out a union?" George answered, "No, Dan, it's above and beyond you, it's administration here and how they treat the staff. It's not in your power." Cynthia discussed how "getting involved at work is a really scary thing," and how she had to overcome feeling worried that people would think badly of her: "That's been my style, to be careful, to be able to get along with everybody. And so for me it was challenging to step outside that and to do that. And also with management who clearly was not appreciative of you wearing a button; [they] stare at your button like you've done something bad just 'cause you're wearing a button." She remembered how the mandatory meetings made her reconsider her decision to become involved:

> I remember walking out of the hospital with [a co-worker] one evening or afternoon after work and after one of these meetings and we both were thinking, "You know what? Maybe this isn't such a good idea, this union stuff. I have to think this through." So we were basically scared off. We thought, "This sounds scary and maybe he's got some points, and it's so controversial."

Frank and Cynthia were two of the relatively well-paid workers who were interested in organizing. Frank "felt confident" he could find work somewhere else if he was fired. Cynthia felt that her husband's job meant that she would not be in dire straits if she were fired. But several workers did not feel so secure. Of the low-wage environmental services (janitorial) employees, Frank remembered, "They would be threatened by their supervisors [that] if they did this they would lose all their benefits, they would lose wages, they may even lose their job. And they could get away with it because they weren't speaking English to them and no one was hearing it."

But the antiunion campaign had effects that went well beyond making particular union leaders feel vulnerable. As the level of tension in the hospital rose, many who had thought the union would be a way to improve the hospital now wondered whether it might in fact be the adversarial force the hospital described. Brandon explained, "Any kind of rumor that goes around or anything management says has an additional layer of credibility or impact that it doesn't normally have because people are just so afraid, or management has made it so clear how much they don't want this to happen." The rhetoric that the hospital used, he continued, "made it very clear that supporting the union means you're against the hospital. That resonates with people in a big way." Brandon recalled that people turned against the union faster than he had ever expected:

> There's this guy I met with who was like, "I'll do whatever it takes, we gotta win this union, I'm down, you can count on me." And then the week before the election he wouldn't even talk to me. Just 'cause the campaign management had run had scared the hell out of people. That stuff is surprising the first time you see it.

Brandon spoke with many members of the organizing committee who told him about "seeing co-workers on one side of the floor who they wanted to talk to, who were supporters, and they would start walking toward them and the person would go walk around the whole other side of the floor to get away from them because they wanted to avoid the whole subject."

In the days leading up to the election Brandon and worker leaders came to the conclusion that they could not win. Support had dropped from 68 percent to less than 50 percent in a matter of a few weeks. This is also sadly typical. In her research on NLRB campaigns, Laura Cooper, a law professor, found that workers had an even chance of winning an election only when union authorization card support reached 62.5 percent.[26] And Cooper's research was conducted two decades before the Memorial campaign, just as employers were developing comprehensive antiunion strategies that made an even higher level of support necessary for winning an election.

As a result of the declining support, SEIU withdrew the petition for an election at Memorial and filed unfair labor practice complaints with the National Labor Relations Board (NLRB). Four months later, in June 2005, after the NLRB documented seven violations of federal labor law, St. Joseph Health System settled with the labor board. Though the system did not admit wrongdoing, it was required to refrain from activities that were illegal under federal law and to post flyers throughout the hospital that stated:

> We will not tell off-duty employees who are engaged in peaceful handbilling to leave the outside nonworking area of our property, nor will we write down the names of off-duty employees engaged in peaceful handbilling who are asked to leave such areas. We will not in any like or related manner interfere with, restrain, or coerce you in the exercise of the rights guaranteed to you by Section 7 of the [National Labor Relations] Act.

But despite this slap on the wrist, management at Santa Rosa Memorial Hospital had won round one of the campaign. Over the next four years the system would face several more sanctions by the NLRB, evidence of its persistent antiunion conduct.

Competing Local Legacies

The union's initial defeat was due, in large part, to the aggressive and comprehensive antiunion campaign waged by hospital management and hired antiunion lawyers. This antiunion campaign was not as nasty as it might have been, however. No union leaders were fired. The hospital did not threaten to close. Rather, through their one-on-one meetings, mandatory group meetings, and literature, managers were able to elevate workers' fears about unionization while downplaying its advantages. This persuasion worked, in part, because there *was* a local example of ineffectual and conflictual unionism from which management could draw: the nearby Sutter Santa Rosa Medical Center. The union, meanwhile, worked to highlight a model of a strong labor-management partnership present at the local Kaiser Santa Rosa Medical Center, but was unable to make this argument successfully.

Sutter Medical Center of Santa Rosa and Kaiser Santa Rosa are the two other main hospitals in Santa Rosa. All three sit within three miles of one another, and at the time of the Santa Rosa Memorial Hospital campaign, both Sutter and Kaiser workers were unionized with UHW. Yet Sutter and Kaiser represented opposite poles of labor-management relations: at Sutter, the union was weak and had been embroiled in battles almost constantly since Sutter had leased the hospital from the county in 1996. Sutter had the reputation for being one of the most vehemently antiunion systems in the state, and it had been engaged in a long and protracted battle with SEIU for years. At Kaiser the union was strong, both in Santa Rosa and around the state. Since 1997 the system had been engaged in an innovative labor-management partnership with SEIU and other unions.[27] For hospital management and antiunion workers, Sutter was suggestive of what might be lost in labor struggle. For union leaders and union supporters, Kaiser was representative of the "union difference."

For hospital management, Sutter Santa Rosa was the archetypical unionized workplace. In the midst of the early campaign at Memorial, in November 2004, both UHW and the CNA announced a one-day strike at Sutter Santa Rosa to protest what they saw as unfair practices during systemwide contract negotiations. This was part of a protracted systemwide struggle that would culminate with the strike that served as my introduction to labor organizing (see the preface).

Yet workers from Sutter Santa Rosa did not seem especially interested in the fight. Only 249 of the 525 workers even voted on whether to participate in the strike, with 206 of them voting in favor. Santa Rosa Memorial Hospital administrators seized on this news, distributing "talking points" to supervisors.[28] One talking point explained that the Sutter facility "told employees that if they strike for one day, they will be replaced [by temporary workers] for the five day minimum period. It is properly referred to as a one day strike with a four day lockout. It is legal. Those who strike for one day will lose five days of pay." Another talking point emphasized that the local had "been in negotiations with Sutter since July." Most important, supervisors were to emphasize that only 30 percent of nurses and 40 percent of ancillary workers authorized the strike, demonstrating "how a majority of employees can lose their voice to a minority with a union and have to pay dues on top of it."

According to a labor organizer who had worked at Sutter Santa Rosa around this time, the union's weakness at the facility was understandable. Before 1996, the hospital was a county-owned public facility known as Community Hospital. In the 1970s and 1980s, as public-sector unionism blossomed across the country, nurses and ancillary workers had established a strong and radical independent union there: "People . . . would go to meetings and there would be like sixty, a hundred people lining the walls."[29] Yet the union's affiliation had changed several times in the recent past, both before and after the hospital's privatization. It became an affiliate of SEIU public sector Local 707, which then merged with Local 1021; and ultimately, through a reorganization of SEIU's California healthcare locals in the early 2000s, it became a member of UHW. At some point during these transitions the nurses decided to break away from the ancillary workers, first as an independent union and then as an affiliate of the California Nurses Association.

As a result of this internal tumult, there was very little enthusiasm for the union and very little in the way of worker leadership. The organizer I interviewed discussed how the union stewards with whom she worked— those workers who play a leadership role—had not been elected, but rather had responded to "a letter in the mail from SEIU [Local] 707 saying that they needed stewards and to call a number if they were interested." The stewards, therefore, "were not leaders" so much as they were a coalition of the willing. What had once been an example of strong, public sector unionism had, by the 2000s, become something of an afterthought for the workers at the hospital and for the union itself. Wages and benefits at Sutter were slightly higher than at Memorial, but not by much.

At Kaiser Santa Rosa the story was entirely different. Workers at Kaiser tended to value the union both for the high wages and generous benefits it secured and for the culture of partnership that it made possible with management. At one point Louise was thinking of leaving Santa Rosa Memorial Hospital and toured the Kaiser facility. She asked workers about the "patient care committees" she had heard about, and they told her, "Oh yeah, we have those, and we definitely work things out about the patients with the management and with the nurses. It's not a thing where they tell you what to do and you do it, the parent-child thing, it's that we work as a group." She spoke with managers who told her they did not "have any problem with the union." When her husband, a Kaiser member, had to be in the hospital in January 2009, Louise looked out the window of his room and saw "somebody standing in front of the nurses and they're making them do these exercises to reduce their stress." When she asked one of the nurses what they were doing, the nurse explained, "Well, it got really busy at the station and everybody was getting really stressed, and somebody came up and said, 'I want you to stop now, stand away from your computers, you're going to do some exercising and break that up.'"

Her experience at Kaiser contrasted sharply with her work at Memorial, where resources were distributed based on Taylorist time-work studies. At Kaiser, "They were more of a 'You can ask us for it, if we have an extra person we're going to bring them over to you, we're not going to go by this acuity system, we're going to give you help when you need it.'" To Louise, Kaiser's twenty-first century labor-management partnership made possible a return to the mid-twentieth-century values she missed at Memorial.

Several other Memorial workers also discussed Kaiser favorably. Mari, who got a job at Kaiser after being laid off from Memorial, believed that at Kaiser workers "are not scared of their immediate supervisors, versus at Memorial they're scared." She also noticed that Kaiser "has their rules" that guide patient care, whereas work at Memorial was always more ad hoc. At Kaiser, she was asked to work only in the labor and delivery department, whereas at Memorial she was often asked to "float to postpartum to help out" when work was slow in labor and delivery. She felt that floating jeopardized the care she could give patients, since floating meant that "sometimes if there is an emergency C-section I don't have the equipment immediately." Furthermore, at Memorial, staffing decisions depended on patient volume. For Mari, this meant that "if I'm due to work at 7 a.m. they can come at 5 a.m. and say sorry we cancelled you." At Kaiser, these sorts of cancellations did not happen. Frank noticed that at Kaiser there was one anesthesia technician for every four rooms; at Memorial, he was responsible for ten patients. George expressed frustration that while respiratory therapists at Memorial have significantly more responsibility than they do at Kaiser, Kaiser's therapists still make much more.

Several Kaiser workers I interviewed corroborated what Memorial workers had told me. April, a chief steward at Kaiser, also worked occasionally at Memorial. At Memorial, she noticed, workers did not seem to have clear roles, and the hospital "cross-train[ed] people that maybe shouldn't be cross-trained." At Kaiser, there were more "skilled workers for appropriate classifications." At Kaiser, a worker knew his or her schedule, whereas at Memorial "it always changes." But the most important difference seemed to be that at Memorial there's "an authoritative structure, and employees are unhappy." Given the arbitrary power that managers had, workers were "scared of retaliation . . . scared to say anything." At Kaiser, workers discussed issues with management on the floor, but at Memorial communication from management was on "bulletin boards." Among Memorial's prounion workers, Kaiser represented what was possible with collective organization.

There were two types of unionism already in existence in Santa Rosa's hospitals—models that served as reference points for both management and labor. In the first round of the Santa Rosa Memorial Hospital unionization campaign, management's analogy prevailed. As suggested above, this was due largely to hospital leadership's control of the debate. But it was also because hospital leadership at Memorial made it crystal clear that they viewed the union as an *adversary*—as power hungry, dues-driven, and ready to go on strike at a moment's notice. In this context, it was difficult to make a convincing case that partnership would ever be possible.

Digging In for the Long Haul

But if the antiunion campaign in late 2004 and early 2005 effectively eroded support for the union among the hospital workers as a whole, it also deepened the resolve and commitment of a core group of leaders, who felt that the ugly face of the hospital had been unveiled. Mari told the story of an interaction she had with a manager in the dietary department. After learning that Mari had been speaking with dietary workers, the manager approached her: "She was so angry at me. [She said,] 'How dare you talk to the employees about that union. You're just scaring them, you know they can lose their jobs, and you can lose your job.'" Mari asked why she should not tell them what she had been hearing. The manager responded, "Well, they're just lucky to have a job. These people are uneducated, they don't know anything." For Mari, "That was my turning point. At that point I was not a hundred percent sure that I was going to get involved, but that morning I realized that I was going to be involved in the union until we get a union." Similarly, Cynthia explained how the hospital's antiunion campaign made her "believe more and more that it would be good for the hospital to have a counterbalance. It was obvious they were acting like a corporation." Dan echoed this sentiment. He was upset by the "lies that they throw out there and the disinformation and the innuendos and some stories I've heard from other departments about the intimidation, real nasty, and the buying of the consultants and all that crap." Dan explained that many workers in his respiratory therapy department had come on board "as they have seen the response to the campaign."

It seems likely that the material benefits of unionization were never what primarily motivated worker leaders.[30] As this chapter suggests, many of those who decided to organize were those motivated by a sense of injustice, and those for whom the values espoused by the hospital resonated most deeply. For this hard-core group of worker leaders, the hospital's concerted antiunion campaign tended to deepen their resolve. Pete discussed how people's involvement in the organizing effort tended to evolve. Although some people fought for the union out of a narrow sense of self-interest "at the beginning," the "campaign creates" something more. And while some workers perhaps "loved going up in front of a room of people and cracking jokes," the people who stuck with it tended to be motivated by something deeper.

As Rick Fantasia has suggested, workers' formal union status may in some ways be less important than the way they learn to act in solidarity with one another over the course of an organizing drive.[31] Even without a contract and its formal protections workers can start *acting* like a union. Rebecca spoke about how a union means "you never have to go before an abusive manager by yourself." Louise thought that most people were involved in the organizing effort because they "want some sort of support," want there to be "people behind you." Yet worker leaders began to provide this support for one another even in the absence of official recognition. On one memorable occasion, José was called in for a meeting with his supervisor in the Nutrition Services Department. Two other members of the organizing committee accompanied him, helping to ensure that the supervisor would not intimidate him.

After the union withdrew its petition in early 2005, the focus of the campaign shifted from the fairly established framework of an NLRB union election to something more ambiguous. Union organizers and workers realized that they would be unable to win an election in the face of concerted management opposition, and so began to campaign for what the union called a "fair election agreement"—a set of ground rules and accountability mechanisms going beyond the National Labor Relations Act that would stave off the kind of campaign the hospital had waged the first time.

According to many labor scholars, current labor law makes it very difficult to organize a union successfully.[32] A report by the labor scholar Gordon Lafer compares labor election law with national election standards, and argues that the secret ballot is the "only point at which current union election procedures met the standards of U.S. democracy."[33] Otherwise, Lafer concludes,

> there is not a single aspect of the NLRB process that does not violate the norms we hold sacred for political elections. The unequal access to voter lists; the absence of financial controls; monopoly control of both media and campaigning within the workplace; the use of economic power to force participation in political meetings; the tolerance of thinly disguised threats; the location of voting booths on partisan grounds; open-ended delays in implementing the results of an election; and the absence of meaningful enforcement mechanisms—every one of these constitutes a profound departure from the norms that have governed U.S. democracy since its inception.[34]

As a solution to the inequalities enshrined in contemporary labor law, unions have sought "fair election agreements" with employers. Under such voluntary agreements, a union and employer typically agree to rules about what each side can say about the other, the access each side has to employees, and the enforcement of the agreed-upon rules. Oftentimes a local mediator is appointed who is able to resolve disputes more quickly than the National Labor Relations Board. Employers, however, tend to regard these agreements as submitting to unionization without a fight. In a meeting in the fall of 2005, Memorial CEO George Perez said that he would not agree to "unilateral disarmament."[35] In 2007, a full-page advertisement by St. Joseph Health System in newspapers up and down California suggested that the union was really lobbying for "front-end agreements that we believe give away the rights of employees to be informed by both sides and to exercise their right to choose in a secret ballot election as outlined by the NLRB."[36]

Political Struggle

In this section I diverge slightly from the chronology of the campaign in order to examine a more standard "social movement union" response to the kind of workplace defeat described above. In their efforts to win "fair election agreements" from employers, unions often search for any conceivable source of economic or political leverage. And in January 2007, a new political opportunity presented itself to those working on the Santa Rosa Memorial Hospital campaign.

On January 8, Sutter Corporation—one of the largest not-for-profit health systems in California—announced that it was closing Sutter Santa Rosa, a hospital that Sonoma County had contracted to Sutter in 1996. The hospital, previously the county's only public hospital, was in need of an expensive seismic retrofit, and it was deeply in the red. Sutter had taken control of the hospital without fully understanding the extent to which indigent patients relied on it. As a result of the closure, Sutter planned to transfer to Santa Rosa Memorial Hospital the "Health Care Access Agreement" it had signed with the county. Under this agreement, Sutter had committed to providing medical services to indigent patients, AIDS patients, and county jail inmates, among other provisions—responsibilities that Memorial would now assume. In turn, Memorial pledged that it would expand its inpatient capacity by eighty beds, expand its urgent care services, and double the size of its emergency department in order to accommodate the new traffic.

The transaction between Sutter and Memorial could not occur, however, without the approval of the Sonoma County Board of Supervisors—something that seemed to go unrecognized by the hospitals and, initially, by the Board of Supervisors itself. The union, however, saw an opportunity to link the fight for the future of the county's healthcare with the organizing struggle at Santa Rosa Memorial Hospital. Specifically, the union hoped that it could prevent Memorial from doing any business with the county unless the hospital agreed to the "fair election agreement." By leading a coalition to place conditions on the proposed transaction, moreover, the union could capitalize on public sentiment against corporate health-care and bring new allies into Memorial's organizing struggle.

This strategy seemed promising at a Board of Supervisors hearing the union helped to organize on February 27, 2007. The hall was packed with hundreds of concerned community members, and many more stood in the adjacent hallway. And unlike other union events, which relied heavily on turnout charts and reminder calls, people seemed to have come to this meeting *spontaneously*.

Yet as the board meeting proceeded, I could see tensions that might emerge for the union. One of the primary concerns among community members concerned Memorial's lack of women's reproductive services. Memorial refuses to administer abortions except in cases of rape and will only perform tubal ligations (or tube-tying) if the procedure can be justified "medically." As Memorial's chief medical officer explained these restrictions, based on Catholic doctrine, there was an audible gasp among the gathered crowd. Yet could the union's theological strategy described below—one premised on building alliances with the Catholic Church—continue if the union was to build alliances with advocates for reproductive services? Even more important, in several hours of audience questions for the Board of Supervisors, almost nothing was said about workers' rights at Memorial. People expressed concerns about care for the poor, emergency room capacity, a family medicine residency program that was based at Sutter, and even helicopter traffic. Aside from five powerful minutes from Father Ray Decker, concern for the workers at either hospital seemed to get lost in the shuffle. After the hearing, a lead organizer on the Memorial campaign assured me that workers' right to organize was the "main peripheral issue"—hardly reassurance at all.

Nevertheless, for the next several months the "healthcare coalition" became the major focus of organizing efforts in Santa Rosa. In April, two political organizers for the union began weekly meetings that brought workers together with Sonoma County healthcare advocates. Ultimately the coalition would come to include several state representatives and other political leaders. In May, the union issued a "Healthcare Justice Platform" that would become the basis of a summerlong petition drive. More than any other document, the platform demonstrated the union's effort to weave together a concern for healthcare in the county with a concern for healthcare *workers*. The first plank of the platform, "Protect and Improve

Healthcare in Sonoma County," demanded a revised "Healthcare Access Agreement" to assure that indigent services would be preserved in the county, and argued that Sutter should remain open until Memorial was able to replace all the services that would be lost. It also advocated for an expansion of primary health clinics in the county and additional funding for several small district hospitals in the county. The second plank, "Be Fair to Those Who Care," advocated on behalf of healthcare workers as well as doctors. It emphasized the need for a plan to ensure smooth job transitions for those being moved from Sutter to Memorial, and made the transaction between Sutter and Memorial contingent on Memorial adopting "fair election" ground rules for its workers interested in unionizing. It also discussed the importance of a vibrant family medicine residency program. Finally, the third plank, "A Community Voice for Healthcare," asked the county to convene a "Citizens healthcare committee" to oversee the planned changes. During the spring and summer, the union spearheaded an effort to gather more than five thousand signatures on the petition. Memorial workers and community advocates collected signatures at grocery stores and farmers' markets. The union also hired a canvassing company to complement the volunteer effort.

And while the political organizers directing the community campaign had initiated it for strategic reasons, according to one leader it "became a mission," a "David versus Goliath fight that we were very proud to be in." These organizers began attending healthcare policy meetings in the county, doing "detective work" and "pounding the pavements." As a result of the information they gleaned, they became informal advisers to the county, and developed personal relationships with several of the county supervisors.

But partly as a result of organizers' missionary zeal, according to one political organizer, the union "lost sight of strategy" in the local fight. It wound up "doing more work in the interests of the community [than] a union should be doing," with little benefit for the Memorial campaign itself. On March 11, 2008, the *Santa Rosa Press Democrat* reported that Sutter, in the face of public pressure, had decided to keep the hospital open.[37] The announcement was tangible proof of the union's political influence, yet a Pyrrhic victory, since the announcement stripped the union of political leverage with Santa Rosa Memorial Hospital. I remember a meeting on the Memorial campaign in late 2008 in which the room seemed filled with local politicians and their aides. One of the community supporters I had worked with turned to me with a look of confusion: "I've never seen so much political support for a local issue. Why can't they do something?" But political influence did not translate into union success—like trying to turn a screw with a hammer.

In narrow political terms, the union's strategy regarding the Sutter-Memorial transaction was unsuccessful. In this political campaign, like the unions in the sociologist Paul Johnston's *Success While Others Fail*, the union sought to frame its claims as "public needs."[38] In his study, Johnston rightly argues that public sector unions operate in a different context than private sector unions: public sector unions are most successful when they make use of "political-organizational resources" and frame their demands in public policy terms,[39] while private sector unions—even at their most creative— tend to use market and political resources to "buttress their market position."[40] This explanation may go some way toward explaining the union's failure to leverage political power in the Santa Rosa Memorial Hospital campaign. The union *was* able to win political power, but it was unable to translate that political power into recognition for the union in the private sector.

Although Johnston's analysis is astute, it fails to make sense of the ideological character of the leadership at Santa Rosa Memorial Hospital. In Johnston's analysis the motivations and strategies of "capital" are assumed away—"the boss is the boss"—and understood as a relatively static "political opportunity structure" to be discerned and taken advantage of.[41] Indeed, the union actually *was* able to translate political pressure into economic pressure over the course of the Sutter campaign, costing Memorial Hospital millions in unnecessary and unfinished construction.[42] But if the union's political campaign "succeeded" to the extent that it prevented the closure of the indigent hospital, cost Santa Rosa Memorial Hospital financially, and likely played a role in the resignation of Memorial's CEO, this economic leverage was not enough to bring Memorial to the negotiating table. As a lead organizer for the union explained, the Sisters of St. Joseph of Orange were *not* motivated solely by economic interests. When the union leveraged its political power to defeat the planned merger, it likely *reinforced* the view among the Sisters that the union was an instrumental actor willing to use almost any means to reach its desired ends.

From a broader perspective, however, the union's work to intervene in the Sutter-Memorial deal, which inadvertently helped lead to its collapse, can be understood as a strategic success. The two political organizers who led the healthcare coalition became trusted colleagues of and advisers to important actors in the local healthcare community. Week after week over the summer of 2007, workers joined with other community members to gather signatures on behalf of the healthcare platform. All of these efforts helped to establish long-term relationships among union leaders, community leaders, and important political actors—and they helped to establish the union as being aligned with the good of the community as a whole. In other places, such as Stamford, Connecticut, labor-community coalitions have successfully blurred the distinction between worker interests and community interests.[43] What may have failed according to the union's narrowest strategic interests may have succeeded in securing the union's long-term reputation within the community and even among workers themselves.

This second interpretation of the campaign against the Sutter-Memorial transaction, however, demands an appreciation of the idea that labor must connect its narrower strategic interests with a broader conception of the public good. It is to this ideological terrain that I now turn. Ultimately it would not be market position but *moral* position that would influence St. Joseph Health System.

A Struggle over New Things

Contesting Catholic Teaching

When I first met Eileen Purcell at a SEIU United Healthcare Workers West convention in 2005, I mistook her for a nun. Her eyes lit up with clarity and fervor as she talked about the Sisters of St. Joseph of Orange. She celebrated these Sisters, who were arrested with the United Farm Workers, who supported the Justice for Janitors campaign, who continued to fight for the poor and access to healthcare, and who worked for peace and an end to war. Yet she was committed to holding these same Sisters accountable for their ongoing opposition to unions. The union convention—boisterous, scripted revelry—seemed odd when juxtaposed with Purcell's theological intensity and her eye for complexity. I struggled to hear Purcell over the convention's music and prerecorded video, which exploded out of loudspeakers over thousands of delegates. Purcell was the sort of person more comfortable singing "This Little Light of Mine" on acoustic guitar.

In 1999, Eliseo Medina, a UFW leader who had joined SEIU in 1996, recruited Fred Ross Jr. to join SEIU's Healthcare Division. Ross recruited Purcell soon afterward, and the two of them worked together out of the international's Oakland office. Together, they were charged with developing SEIU's "Catholic Strategy," an approach to organize the largely non-union Catholic hospital industry. SEIU believed that it could ultimately reach a "national settlement" with Catholic hospitals. In an internal memo, the union discussed "developing a coherent industry-wide strategy to sharpen employers' choice between strategic alliances with the union *and* traditional labor-management confrontational/adversarial relations when they refuse to listen to and work with their work force."[1]

SEIU had already had significant success in isolated Catholic systems. In 2001, for example, it had won an important organizing agreement with Catholic Healthcare West in California and had established contracts at twenty-eight of that system's hospitals. According to the internal memo, however, the current organizing efforts were "not significant enough for the systems or political/religious allies to come to a table and resolve conflicts or generate national settlement. Most employers have conducted cost benefit analyses and believe they can hold out." Indeed, notwithstanding the successful collaboration between SEIU and CHW following the bitter struggle leading to that election agreement, most of Catholic healthcare viewed the agreement as a betrayal of industry interests. In order to reach a breakthrough nationwide, union leaders concluded, "We need to build to crisis while holding up positive alternatives." According to international leaders, a breakthrough at another two Catholic systems within the top ten largest systems (of which St. Joseph Health System was one) would likely create a tipping point within Catholic healthcare nationwide.

Ross began devoting significant time to the Santa Rosa Memorial Hospital campaign soon after the local withdrew its election petition in early 2005. SJHS was one of the few Catholic systems at which workers were already mobilized, and the only nonunion system in which the religious leadership had agreed to speak face-to-face with union representatives. The leadership of Saint Joseph Health System was also closely linked to others in the Catholic healthcare world. The former CEO of St. Joseph Health System had become CEO of the Bon Secours Health System, a large Catholic system headquartered in Maryland. Through its board of directors, SJHS was connected with several other large Catholic systems as well.

For its part, the local SEIU-UHW also had an interest in expanding the Memorial campaign across the entire system. St. Joseph Health System is headquartered in Orange County, California, an area of Southern California where the union had comparatively low density. Getting in the door at Memorial would likely have repercussions down south. So while the local and international had had disagreements in the past, the SJHS campaign was a point of convergence. In the years after the local withdrew its election petition, union staff dedicated to the systemwide campaign would increase tenfold and would expand to encompass seven of the system's thirteen hospitals.

Yet in almost all of the "fair election agreement" campaigns that unions had led within Catholic health systems in the past, economic and political leverage were integral parts. At Catholic Healthcare West, the union threatened to lobby the Democratic-controlled state legislature to repeal legislation that permitted the hospital system to retrofit its hospitals gradually for seismic safety. As one organizer told me, this legislative change "was going to cost billions of dollars," whereas "an increase in labor costs is never going to be that much, ever." A deal struck with the floundering Caritas Christi Health Care in Boston traded organizing rights for a commitment by the union to lobby for increases in state funding for the system.[2] Other efforts by SEIU in Ohio, Oregon, and New York—and by AFSCME in Illinois—also sought to leverage economic and legislative power.[3]

St. Joseph Health System, on the other hand, was in good shape financially, and so was relatively immune to the economic and political leverage that the union might muster. Rather, the union would have to use moral leverage, "elevating the Sisters' strong legacy supporting the rights of farm workers, janitors, and immigrants in sharp contrast to their opposition to SJHS workers' efforts to unionize."[4] The Sisters of St. Joseph of Orange had one of the most progressive legacies of any hospital system sponsor. As one union memo put it, "The sisters' greatest strength—their legacy in favor of social and worker justice—was also their greatest vulnerability, given the serious, documented disconnect between their words and deeds at SJHS."[5] Unlike almost any other hospital executive or owner in the country, the chairwoman of St. Joseph Health System's board of directors had agreed to sit down with SEIU representatives on several occasions. Purcell recognized the rarity of this willingness: "You're dealing with genuine soul searching and struggling. And I have to say what set Sister Kit [Gray] apart is that she was willing to engage and dialogue." But over the course of the SJHS campaign it began to seem that system leaders were using dialogue itself as a tactic to avoid unionization—"dialoguing to death," as one union leader put it, without changing its practices.

The centerpiece of the union's campaign thus shifted from the workplace to the religious arena. The union would seek to convince the Sisters that they had a moral obligation to allow their workers a "free and fair union election." The Sisters would seek to reconcile their position on unions with Catholic teaching. The primary audience for this back-and-forth became the wider Catholic community of which the Sisters were a part.

Catholic Support for the Rights of Workers

The Church's support for labor unions harkens back to Pope Leo XIII's 1891 encyclical on "The Rights and Duties of Capital and Labour," known more formally as *Rerum Novarum* (or "of new things"). The document, written at a time when the Catholic Church was losing its moral and intellectual centrality in the world, put the church forward as a mediator between labor and capital, and argued that the labor union was the best compromise between the two, a way to ensure the dignity of working people while protecting the private property on which the foundations of society must be based. The Pope recognized that "working men have been surrendered, isolated and helpless, to the hardheartedness of employers and the greed of unchecked competition," but dismissed the socialist solution. Collective state ownership was equivalent to theft, and toward this "the authority of the divine law adds it sanction, forbidding us in severest terms even to covet that which is another's." The labor union—like the "artificers' guilds of olden times"—would protect workers' livelihood at the same time that it would preserve their spirit, so long as these unions were not "managed on principles ill-according with Christianity and the public well-being."

The Church's somewhat ambivalent stance toward worker power—supporting unions at least in part out of fear of something *worse*—is reflected in a complicated history of the Church's involvement in the U.S. labor movement.[6] Nevertheless, in recent years—perhaps in response to the *decline* of radical labor organizing, and the further expansion of free-market capitalism—the Catholic Church has affirmed its support for labor unions more unambiguously. In 1981, in *Laborem Exercens* ("On Human Work"), Pope John Paul II argued that workers have a right "to form associations for the purpose of defending the vital interests of those employed in the various professions." He also argued that the labor union should be understood "as a normal endeavor 'for' the just good . . . not a struggle 'against' others." In 1986, the U.S. Catholic bishops asserted in a pastoral letter on the economy, "No one may deny the right to organize without attacking human dignity itself." Moreover, they argued that the "purpose of unions is not simply to defend the existing wages and pre-rogatives of the fraction of workers who belong to them, but also to enable workers to make positive and creative contributions to the firm, the community, and the larger society in an organized and cooperative way."

Joseph Fahey, a professor of religion at Manhattan College and founder of Catholic Scholars for Worker Justice, became an asset to workers and union leaders during the St. Joseph Health System campaign. He inter-preted Catholic social teaching on unions as meaning that Catholic em-ployers should "encourage their workers to organize." *Human rights* in Catholic thought are not to be "passively acknowledged," he said in an interview, but rather "should be positively fostered." He continued, "If you have a right to vote, people shouldn't say, 'Well, then, you have a right not to vote. . . .' You have the right to vote, you should vote." And while civil law may require employers to be neutral, he wrote, "I believe Catholic em-ployers should not sit on that fence. No, Catholic employers should adopt a Quaker 'ethic of welcome' regarding unions. That is, workers should be told by Catholic employers that they welcome unions as a sign of faith-fulness to Catholic social teaching."[7] Unions were not just a means to an end—a protection against a bad workplace—but rather were "an end in themselves, because unions foster solidarity and association," values that are recognized as important in Catholic thought. For him, "any corporate model in which there are owner/managers and non-union/employees ne-cessitates a union on the part of workers so that they may bargain collec-tively rather than individually for their rights."[8]

This idea—that union membership was desirable under any circum-stances—was widespread among union leaders. One union leader said that she "has to believe" that people who are members of unions are better off than those who are not. She observed that while "any human institution is flawed," without unions workers are screwed "because we're dealing with power and control issues. And the reflex of management is to balance their budgets on the backs of workers." A corporation was a corporation, regardless of the service it provided or the religious values it espoused.

Many of the organizers with whom I worked had little interest in healthcare or Catholicism before joining UHW, but rather had come to work for the union because of its reputation for advocating strongly and militantly on behalf of workers' rights. Brandon, the lead organizer on the Memorial campaign, was inspired to work in the labor movement by the 2001 general strikes in Argentina, where he was studying abroad. He took part in a "Union Summer" program after returning to the United States, and when he went back to school that fall he fought a successful campaign at his college to institute a living wage policy for service workers. Upon graduation, he took a job with Local 250 because he heard it would be a "good place to learn how to organize," but not because "he wanted to work with healthcare workers." Pete, the lead political organizer on the campaign, had gotten active in labor issues in college, where he created a student-labor alliance in support of the International Longshore and Warehouse Union (ILWU). For each of them, a commitment to workers came before a commitment to healthcare.

Perhaps at least in part as a result, organizers often spoke of all "workers" at the hospital in one breath, despite the radically different job classifications and pay scales within the bargaining units that were being organized. During one staff meeting regarding efforts to expand the campaign into a St. Joseph Health System hospital in a neighboring county, the organizing director of the union said that while the technical and professional employees he visited may have lived in nice houses, they identified as "workers" nonetheless. If you live in the community around the hospital, he explained, "you know you're not rich because you don't own a winery." For him, it seemed, all employees' relationships to their bosses shared similar characteristics, regardless of their specific pay scales or positions.

As the union and its supporters sought to make their case in the religious community, they highlighted the declining role of sisters in the daily operation of the facility, implying that the Sisters had ceded theological authority to business-oriented managers. At one point in time, the Sisters of St. Joseph of Orange both managed and made up most of the staff within their hospitals. But as "labor priest" Monsignor George G. Higgins observed of contemporary Catholic hospitals, "the men and women who . . .

work in the kitchens of our Catholic hospitals . . . have not volunteered to serve the church."[9] Among management at Memorial, the union suggested, a business ethic has filled the vocational void. One Catholic priest noticed, "You go there to Memorial you wouldn't find a nun in there. You might find one floating around as a chaplain, but that place used to be filled with nuns." A labor leader added: "The stalwarts were the women religious, and they're getting old and dying. And so these institutions remain and they're being led by people whose culture is largely the business culture."

According to many religious leaders supportive of the union, Sister Katherine Gray and the sisters leading the hospital had become pawns of the business side of the healthcare system. One priest observed, "She's got all these people that are making six-figure salaries that are advising her and saying, 'Unions are going to bring down this hospital system, they're going to destroy it,' so she's trying to walk a tightrope." Another priest recalled speaking to Sister Katherine about her position on unions. She had responded, "I will listen to my advisers." This priest remembered thinking, "So that's where I say, 'What is it that's supposed to really advise you? Your spirituality and your social teaching.'" A third priest suggested that the sisters' loyalty to their hospitals had meant they had come to depend on business expertise in order to keep them strong: "What they've done to manage this whole situation [is] they've had to hire all these laypeople, and these people come out of a business structure, so many of them come out of an antiunion business structure, so they've turned a lot of the actual administration over to them." According to this priest, the Sisters' divestment from the active administration of the hospital was reflective of broader changes in the healthcare system that made the market unavoidable:

> They're in the market system. And that's what makes the union all the more important, is to fight out that in the market system, the rights of employees, to equalize that situation out. You can't be a multibillion-dollar corporation and contend you're not in the market system.

Religious leaders tended to see the Sisters as serving little more than a symbolic role at the hospital, espousing religious values that belied their corporate practices. One priest argued that the Sisters "have had to develop a vocabulary and a propaganda mechanism in order to defend the way they are." According to one union leader, some priests went so far as to suggest "there are no longer Catholic hospitals" at all, with their religious values emptied entirely of meaning. Similarly, Brandon saw the system's hired ethicist as having almost no autonomy from the prerogatives of management: "[He] provides a justification for whatever the company wants to do. There's no other PhDs in theology [around], [so] no one's gonna tell [the ethicist] he's wrong 'cause no one knows anything about it." He thought that it was no coincidence that the system's rhetoric on unions varied "little from the standard antiunion line from the Chamber of Commerce or the National Right to Work committee or any other normal private sector employer."

Nevertheless, among union organizers, the challenge was to elevate the Sisters' legacy and challenge them to take a more active role in shaping the everyday practices within their hospitals. This made organizers' perspectives differ slightly from their religious supporters. Where religious leaders suggested that the market for healthcare had vanquished the Sisters' capacity to lead, organizers pointed out that the Sisters remained at the helm, at least formally, and that the Sisters struggled with the tension between their values and the business of running a hospital. Indeed, it was this tension that provided the union with the possibility of moral suasion. Purcell noted that while the hospital was a business, "there are some sisters monitoring the mission, or aspiring to, who act out of that charism. And that has a softening impact, that has a pastoral dimension that is part of the culture, that is different from a for-profit hospital." When I asked Ross whether he thought the Sisters were like any other executives or whether they were susceptible to religious argument, he answered, "They're both." Brandon believed that among the religious leadership there was "a certain amount of self-delusion going on." He suggested that these leaders "also understand that a union means they lose power and it's worse to them to lose power than to do something they might have to do some mental acrobatics around to rationalize." But he contrasted these religious leaders with the business-minded local CEO at Memorial who could "go run a factory someplace and be just as happy."

One male organizer of Catholic faith went so far as to suggest that the Sisters struggled with a kind of "internalized colonization." As women in the church, the Sisters had been "treated as second-class citizens." As a result, they "then say screw you all, including the male hierarchy of the church," and argue that they "know what's best for the workers." The paradox was that the Sisters had come to embody the same paternalism that has subordinated them within the Church: "They actually become what they hate." Another union leader offered a less psychoanalytic perspective. For her, Catholic institutions—including women's religious orders—had always been hierarchical "in their bones and structure and architecture and governance structures. . . . You still have vows of obedience." This leader asked rhetorically, "Did they ever believe in worker voice? I don't think so."

A Different Frame

Leaders of St. Joseph Health System rejected the charge that they were antiunion, although they did ultimately acknowledge—after sanctions from the NLRB—that their behavior in Santa Rosa in 2005 had been inappropriate. One system ethicist acknowledged that there had been times when the system "conducted campaigns in a shameful way." Another system executive suggested that the *Fair Election Commission Report* produced by the union after it had withdrawn its election petition in 2005, and supported by prominent local religious leaders, had drawn the hospital system's attention to the union question: "When there was a group of people alleging a certain set of behaviors on our part, I think we stepped back and said, 'We need to look at that.'" Union leaders pointed out, however, that this report did not change the system's antiunion practice in significant ways over the next four years.

In addressing the question of unionization, system leadership disputed the idea that they represented a "powerful organization" in opposition to a "voiceless worker." As one ethicist put it, "I came to realize through study, through research, and through discernment that that is not the landscape of this issue. The landscape is, there is a healthcare organization with power, there are unions with power. And there are two voices of employees, some employees who want [a union], and employees who don't want [it]. So for me, that's the landscape." The ethical question for him was how to create an environment in which workers could choose without being unduly influenced by *either* organization.

According to one union leader, however, equating the hospital with the union as two equally powerful organizations "assumes that workers are vulnerable to the union in this equal way that workers [are vulnerable to employers.]" The hospital "hires and fires them and assigns them their schedule and has power over them," whereas the union has none of this authority. Equating the hospital and the union denied the "power relationship" that existed within the hospital.

But for hospital leaders, the union and its supporters were too dogmatic in their advocacy for unions under any circumstances. While expressing its support for unions and affirming the rights of workers to organize, the *Compendium of the Social Doctrine of the Church*, for example, also argued that unions "must overcome the temptation of believing that all workers should be union-members."[10] One system executive explained how she had come to see that some union leaders and supporters believed "there cannot be a fair and just workplace without a union, that there is an inherent unfairness in the manager relationship. I don't believe that; that's certainly not a position that I share."

A second ethicist argued that theologians such as Joseph Fahey were "fundamentalist in their approach," in that they took "a limited set of texts" and interpreted them too literally. Rather than draw narrowly on those teachings on the rights of workers to organize, ethicists within the health system argued that they "were really looking at a larger body of theological stuff that had to do with work, the workplace, human dignity, growth, civic responsibility, and then kind of trying to see the issues of unions and union elections in that kind of a context."

This position was fleshed out more fully by Jack Glaser, an ethicist during the early stages of the Santa Rosa Memorial Hospital campaign and the chief architect of SJHS's early position regarding unionization. Glaser had been with St. Joseph Health System since 1986, and was a progressive voice on U.S. healthcare reform. In an article titled "Fruit on the Diseased Tree of U.S. Healthcare,"[11] he argued that Catholic hospitals cannot be in keeping with religious dictates without systemic healthcare reform. By analogy he wrote of the efforts of a colony of Mennonites who sought to renounce slavery in South Carolina in the seventeenth century, only to leave in failure. Just as the colony failed, Catholic healthcare could not be true to its values and sustain itself within the "parameters of organizations within . . . society." In a separate piece for the CHA, Glaser argued that while "most Americans implicitly frame healthcare as a commodity, a market good . . . in all other developed countries and in Catholic social teaching, health care is recognized as a social good—an indispensable good required for the flourishing of society and the individuals in it."[12] From 2002 to 2009, Glaser helped to lead the system's Center for Healthcare Reform, and was quoted as having argued that "dysfunctional ethics on the societal level have cascaded down into our Catholic health care ministry in such a way that makes it almost impossible to carry out our ministry in any respectable manner."[13]

Yet Glaser was opposed to unionization efforts in St. Joseph Health System hospitals, and he developed a theological argument for the system's antiunion efforts. According to Glaser, the question facing any Catholic organization is whether, in that particular workplace, a union offers a greater or lesser probability of moving toward a "Biblical" workplace.[14] Responding to the body of Catholic social teaching that expounds on the virtues of unions, he argued that unions tend to use church teachings as "battle quotes," which were "simple; brief; [and] narrowly focused." He suggested that this body of teaching was actually "layered; elaborate; and expansive." Glaser believed that a workplace is "a community, a network of systems and structures that serve sacredness of dignity"; that work is "an essential way that holy and sacred dignity grows to fullness."[15] The starting point for evaluating a workplace should be whether it makes dignity possible. He went on to elaborate what distinguished "good" from "bad" workplaces, as well as "good" from "bad" unions. A good workplace, he implied, may justly work to keep out a "bad" union. This idea was echoed by SJHS's CEO Deborah Proctor, who argued that Catholic social teaching "doesn't start out talking about unions, it starts by talking about the dignity of the person. That's the primary principle of Catholic social teaching."[16]

Among workers and union leaders, the system's promise to promote workplace dignity struck a hollow chord. Furthermore, for Fahey, Glaser's theological position was "dishonest" and "a really fraudulent presentation of Catholic teaching." Purcell maintained that the Glaser paradigm was flawed on at least three counts. First, it failed to acknowledge the power differential between management and workers. Second, it failed to honor workers' right to decide for themselves whether or not to unionize. Third, it held a truncated view of unions, which limited their function to protecting against abusive employers and negotiating for wages, benefits, and working conditions. For Purcell, unions were about a broader conception of economic citizenship and social justice.

About Glaser himself, Fahey believed, "he's dangerous. And these nuns, frankly, they sit and listen. They hear what they want to hear." They weren't the only ones. Rumors were that Glaser's PowerPoint presentation on unions in Catholic hospitals had been in demand across the country.

The Mission-Driven Workplace

Hospital system leaders did not admit to being antiunion. Rather, they consistently affirmed that they "preferred a direct relationship" with their employees over unionization. This phrase had been used as a euphemism for antiunionism in other systems as well, but it also accurately conveyed hospital leaders' hesitancy about the union. For them, a union would threaten the organization's capacity to be oriented toward its mission. According to one Sister on the SJHS board, "We want people to experience the workplace as a community, as teams focused on the mission, patient care, and care for one another." A union, she implied, would make this more difficult. Another executive said that her biggest challenge was "organizational alignment . . . having one vision and moving everybody towards that vision and ministry together." She suggested that the "nature of the [union-management] relationship tends to be one of defensiveness [as opposed to] alignment." This was not necessarily the case, she continued, yet she thought that by its very nature a union "seems to create a chasm to begin with." An ethicist within the system suggested that a union generated "loyalty within the subgroup, that needs to be there for that to have a meaningful life of its own." But this loyalty, he implied, would distract from the organization's greater purpose.

This explanation for antiunionism has special resonance within the world of Catholic healthcare. Historically, the nun had been a prototype for the selfless caregiver, and this selflessness was important for the development of Catholic hospitals. When sisters were actively running and administering hospitals, spiritual formation fostered "submission and obedience," which in turn "enabled the motherhouse to apply the human resources of the community expeditiously."[17] A belief in the importance of self-subordination—of the martyred heart—has had important symbolic effects long after nuns withdrew from active nursing practice. Extended to the present, it implies that financial considerations sully the motivations of caregivers. In 2002, *Health Progress*, the journal of the Catholic Health Association (CHA), dedicated an entire issue to the problem of labor. In an especially revealing piece, Sister Patricia Talone argued that traditional Catholic teaching on unions is irrelevant to Catholic healthcare:

> After all, a Catholic health care organization does not merely deliver a product; it commits itself to a ministry. The primary object of a Catholic health care organization is not primarily financial gain, but the care of the poor, sick, and vulnerable; it seeks financial strength to serve the ministry.[18]

As a result, in Catholic healthcare, "the usual employer/employee dichotomy is replaced by a community of people dedicated to working together toward a common goal."[19] When there are "contentious arguments" between management and employees in such organizations, "people both inside and outside the ministry are often dismayed and discouraged."[20] The union sets up a class dichotomy where there should be harmony, and replaces selflessness with self-interest. Privately, the Sisters worried that a union would replace covenants with contracts, that it would reduce the hospital's mission to a set of rules. One ethicist worried that a union would "formalize and juridicize things that don't need that." A nun who met with Sister Katherine Gray reported that Gray worried that a union would ruin the good relationship that existed between workers and managers.

St. Joseph Health System, like many businesses, asserts a set of "values" toward which it strives: "Dignity, Excellence, Service, and Justice." Unlike other businesses, however, the system has at each of its hospital facilities a department dedicated solely to "mission integration," or ensuring the consistency of the system's practices with the Catholic values on which it was founded. The system also has hired "ethicists" who apply Vatican-issued directives on Catholic healthcare and, more generally, helped translate Catholic teaching into practice.

SJHS leadership seemed to understand these values as needing protection from the adversarial, contractual practices of labor unions. When workers first started organizing at Memorial in late 2004, it was the hospital's director of mission integration who led compulsory antiunion meetings for all staff. She suggested that the union would undermine otherwise harmonious relationships between managers and workers. This was a conception shared widely among administrators in Catholic healthcare.

Memorial CEO George Perez stated that his duty was "to educate employees about what a union will do to the hospital, how it will upset our
family."[21]

The Sisters' experiences of labor organizing drives in Catholic hospitals
reaffirmed this belief. According to Purcell, who had been in contact with
over thirty sisters to explore bridging the divide between organized labor
and Catholic healthcare, "At the CHA annual convention, the union was
cast as one of several forces threatening Catholic healthcare's survival."[22]
The relationship between sisters and this healthcare union had some history, of course. The confrontational tactics employed during the previous
campaign at CHW had alienated sisters from SEIU. The campaign had
been long and drawn out, though at the end the system agreed to a preelec-
tion agreement, most workers in the system elected to unionize, and SEIU
and CHW embarked on developing a working partnership. Nevertheless,
after the campaign the relationship between the union and hospital management was significantly more collegial than the relationship between the
union and the sisters who had been involved in the struggle:

> Many women religious sponsors and lay managers viewed the CHW-SEIU
> settlement as a betrayal of Catholic healthcare systems. CHW sponsors them-
> selves remained highly critical for years after the protracted, system-wide
> organizing drive at their hospitals—even after settlement was achieved and
> an effective and creative labor-management relationship was put in place—
> and supported their counterparts' resistance to unionization.[23]

One religious leader in the Memorial campaign knew friends of Sister
Katherine Gray and attested she was "shaken to the roots" by the union's
theological strategy:

> Some very legitimate people have said, "You're way off base here." And
> when people keep telling her that, "You're way off base here, there's some-
> thing wrong with you, you're not functioning right," well, you can only take
> that so long. You begin to doubt the way you've been thinking.

Whereas both labor and management had understood the campaign as
something of a contest, many of the Sisters had felt personally and more
lastingly wounded, experiencing the union's strategy as an ad hominem
attack.[24] One organizer consistently demonstrated this tension within the

union between its theological rhetoric and more adversarial stance. In public, and with religious leaders, he would speak in moral language about the Sisters' honorable legacy and the "disconnect" between their values and their antiunion practices. In private, however, he assumed a crasser stance when he felt that the hospital leaders were betraying workers' rights: "Stick it to them, fucking assholes," he growled on more than one occasion.

Union organizers did disrupt the status quo, but from their perspective they did not *introduce* an adversarial employment relationship so much as provide a counterbalance to an adversarial power relationship that already existed. The union was necessary precisely because workers did not feel they had the kind of reciprocal relationship with the Sisters that a "direct relationship" implied. In a meeting I helped to arrange between my father, Robert Reich (Secretary of Labor during President Clinton's first term), Sister Katherine, and SJHS CEO Deborah Proctor, Reich suggested that a "direct relationship" might actually be *more* possible with a union than without, so that workers could have a voice that is not silenced by power differences in the workplace.[25] Certainly, an environment that management describes as harmonious can be experienced quite differently by workers themselves.[26]

That being said, even within the labor movement there is some history to the idea that vocational commitment is inconsistent with unionization. Where union supporters publicly espoused the mobilized heart—that unionization would allow workers the opportunity to reclaim the mission of the hospital—unions have traditionally fostered the martyred heart among their own staffs. Suzanne Gordon has documented the prevalent antiunionism of unions when their own staff members tried to organize,[27] articulated most clearly by the former organizer and contemporary labor scholar Lance Compa: "You're working to serve the membership . . . so it's inherently a conflict of interest to act in an adversarial manner that involves the use of strikes or pressure tactics to . . . interfere with the workings of the union." For him, the important question was "whether [your work is] just a job or whether you consider yourself as belonging to a movement that has a broader social meaning. . . . And that kind of movement requires dedication and the ability to resolve conflicts as colleagues and comrades, not as adversaries or enemies."[28] Compa would go on to become the author of the influential Human Rights Watch report *Unfair Advantage: Workers' Freedom of Association in the United States under Human Rights Standards.*[29]

At the very least, Compa's articulation of the inconsistency between vocational commitment and unionization suggests that the martyred heart is not foreign to union organizers themselves. In a revealing moment, Pete asked, "Why do organizers work the amount of hours they do for the pay they get? I think it has a piece of faith to it."

Outside Agitators

Another widespread belief among St. Joseph Health System leaders was that the union was a "third party" made up of people other than the workers themselves. In response, union leaders pointed out that workers at Memorial had called the union—the union did not begin the campaign uninvited. More generally, however, union leaders argued that social movements are rarely sparked without "outsiders" recruiting, training, and developing leaders—an idea supported by the social movement literature.[30] Ross put the point succinctly:

> Planting seeds is not illegitimate. UAW went in to organize auto, right? Cesar [Chavez] went into Delano. It wasn't like thousands of farmworkers sent letters to Cesar and said, "Please come organize us." Yeah, you go out, you evangelize, you plant seeds, and there's either interest or there isn't. But a fundamental principle for us, there's gotta be worker interest and leadership. That's what's gonna drive it.

Despite these arguments, there was something of a divide between union staffers and worker leaders in the Memorial campaign, which occasionally created a degree of tension. During my experience with the union there were often at least two levels of meetings that took place before workers had input into strategy: a meeting between the organizing director and other lead organizers (often in Oakland), and a meeting between the lead organizers and the other staff organizers. Even in the weekly organizing committee meetings with worker leaders, workers often sat around a large square table while a staff organizer stood at the front. The organizer would have written the agenda beforehand, often with little room for spontaneous participation.[31] It is not necessarily surprising that a large labor organization would sometimes take on the trappings of bureaucracy, but these bureaucratic tendencies did come into tension with the conception of the union as an organization that made possible worker voice.

And while the union did not want to be seen as outsiders, most of those who worked for the union *were* outsiders to some extent. Nearly every staff person on the campaign drove to Santa Rosa from San Francisco or the East Bay. Mari described how the union "changed people like socks," as organizers were hired on to the campaign or left to work somewhere else. The feeling of being an outsider hit home for me on a cloudy afternoon before a press conference at Santa Rosa Memorial Hospital for which I was responsible. I suddenly realized that although I had worked on the campaign for almost six months, I had spent almost all of my time working in the local religious community and I had no idea how to get to the facility. Another community organizer and I spent almost fifteen minutes driving around town before we found our bearings.

In their discussions of union strategy, St. Joseph Health System leaders implied that workers did not *really* desire a union. This was not true, although support for unionization emerged organically in some places and was more carefully developed and amplified in others. In Santa Rosa, workers had always been the leaders of the campaign, but as the "fair election" campaign moved statewide in 2007 there was not the same kind of spontaneous support. In February 2007, with the leadership of Glenn Goldstein, the union organized a "blitz" of workers in the system's three hospitals in Orange County. For three days, two hundred union staffers and members contacted workers at their homes in teams of two, looking for those few workers who might be able to lead the organizing efforts. The metaphor that one union organizer used was that of "mining for diamonds."

Since wages and benefits were not of great concern to many employees within St. Joseph Health System, we were trained by union leaders to search for stories that would highlight the need for a union outside of the standard wage and benefit concerns. In a section of the training entitled "tough questions," we spent several minutes discussing how to respond to a worker if he or she said, "I love my job." The correct response, we learned, was to say, "That's great. What do you love about it?" The goal was to get the person to open up about his or her work, and then ask, "Is there anything you'd want to change about your job?" At another morning meeting, we spent a good deal of time discussing how to respond to workers if they said that their workplace is "like a family."

For St. Joseph Health System, this kind of targeting proved that union staff was promoting discord where previously there had been harmony. For the union, on the other hand, these sorts of systemwide campaigns were just good strategy. Moreover, union leaders argued, support often exists well before it is visible, as the Arab Spring movements for democratization demonstrated in 2011. Organizing only those "hot shops" with spontaneous worker leadership would never be enough to reverse labor's decline.[32] During the door-knocking drive, several "diamonds" had emerged. And soon afterward, organizers put together a meeting for all these supporters. Ross spoke of that first meeting as "quite an emotional experience." He saw that the "big elephant in the room was worker fear." Workers had the desire to organize, he remembered, but anticipated an aggressive counter-campaign from management. Anticipating this reaction, organizers had made sure that worker leaders from Santa Rosa were present to offer "encouragement and hope" to these relative newcomers. Andrew, a unit secretary and one of the strongest leaders from Memorial, discussed how he had been afraid too. But he went on to tell the others "how good it felt to put my pro-union flyer right in George Perez's [Memorial's CEO] face." Ross recalled "huge peals of laughter, 'cause people could see themselves doing that to their CEO." At another moment in the meeting, when an organizer explained to worker leaders how publicly supporting the union gave you legal rights that silent support would not, "a light bulb clicked on and this one worker jumped up and said, 'I get it! Norma Rae!'"

Given a broader context in which the labor movement has been declining in power and influence for two generations, should we really expect rank-and-file leadership to emerge from the ether?

The Just Workplace

St. Joseph Health System leaders and the Sisters themselves downplayed workers' independent interest in unionization. An admission of workers' interest, it seemed, would mean that leaders had not been proper stewards; it would be an admission that Catholicism had lost its centrality within the system. One system ethicist said that employees' interest in unionization would indicate "that somehow there's something in the workplace that our folks feel they're going to be better represented by somebody that they don't even know right now, than by the supervisors and the administration and the structures of the organization." For him, workers' interest in unionization "should become a kind of a wake-up call." In a local newspaper article, the hospital's vice president of human resources suggested that employees had actually *resisted* unionization because of "the spirit of the people who come to work here. People come here not just to work in health care, but to work in a Catholic, nonprofit system. We encourage a safe, open environment where we can talk to one another, and we are very committed to doing that."[33] Support for the union, she implied, would mean the hospital system had failed to create this kind of environment.

One priest, who had previously served on the board of a St. Joseph Health System hospital, discussed how "the hospital looked upon unions as the black plague and took it as a personal affront: 'You mean to tell me that we're not taking good care of you? Why do you have to have somebody else looking out for your benefits when we are looking out so well for you?'" This perspective—that support for the union was an indictment of the Sisters' capacity to sustain their own values—was one that hospital leaders shared with many Catholic allies who *did* support the campaign. A Catholic deacon who supported the organizing drive at Memorial argued that "the way to avoid a union is to eliminate the need for one, and the way you eliminate the need for one is to manage your company with the people in mind and not just your own gain." A former Sister of St. Joseph of Orange thought that the Sisters still wanted "to be the ones that will hear the workers and do for the workers. . . . I don't believe that there are mechanisms [for this] or workers wouldn't be asking for a union."

In some ways St. Joseph Health System actually was a good employer compared to other hospital systems and did engage in some indisputably charitable endeavors. During one of my first days working for the union, I accompanied my boss as we met with the union's video producer. The producer had very specific ideas about what kinds of stories would be powerful in a piece: in a video made for another hospital, he had interviewed a woman who was homeless because she could not afford to pay rent given her low hospital pay; in another video, he interviewed a man who had to live in Tijuana and commute across the border to work at a Southern California hospital. Yet these stories just did not exist at Santa Rosa Memorial Hospital. As we urged the producer to frame the video around the rights of workers to have a "voice" at work, and the inconsistency of SJHS's anti-unionism with Catholic social teaching, the producer interjected:

> You know, we should try to get a Hispanic to talk about being an immigrant, ideally this person would speak in Spanish, talk about being an immigrant, taking citizenship classes, trying to make ends meet, and having a hard time because he or she isn't being paid well enough at the hospital.

These sorts of stories were not common at Memorial, however, a hospital at which the staff was largely white and fairly well compensated.

According to one hospital executive, over the course of the campaign religious leaders had approached him with the impression that the system was "paying terrible wages and don't give [employees] benefits." When he showed them "what we pay the people who work in our housekeeping departments and our dietary departments and our service departments and the level of benefits that they had," these religious leaders changed their perspective: "Their feeling that they had to come in to protect the workers just kind of went away."

In another revealing moment, the union held a staff meeting at which a group of organizers discussed the system's community outreach team. St. Joseph Health System had hired six organizers to work on pastoral outreach, which included advocating on behalf of immigrants—an issue that took on particular importance during the immigrant rights rallies in the spring and fall of 2007. In the middle of the meeting, the union's organizing director turned to the rest of the staff and said—half jokingly—"Why'd we pick this target again?" Talking about union strategy regarding St. Joseph Health System, a different organizer said in an interview:

> You have companies like Tenet Health and the way we broke those guys was we helped expose the fact they were performing unnecessary bypasses on people, totally fraudulent heart surgeries, they're cracking people's chests for no good reason.

But St. Joseph Health System had not been doing "anything that everyone else isn't doing," he suggested, meaning that it was less vulnerable to the sorts of public campaigns that the union had engaged in against other hospital systems.

For union allies, however, the issue was not so much about wages or benefits as about workers being entitled to respect. According to one union leader, St. Joseph Health System believed "unions are exclusively to protect workers from bad actors." For her, "unions have a much larger vision. They're part of not only the bread and butter issues but good citizenship, economic citizenship, civil rights movements, immigrant rights movements." Within the campaign, she continued, "we were facilitating workers claiming their role in the institution as stakeholders who love their work, loved the Sisters of old, but wanted greater voice." Indeed, without this voice, it was difficult to tell how workers really felt at all. In his meeting with hospital leaders, Robert Reich told them, "Managers always want to believe workers are more satisfied than they are." He suggested that when workers are powerless they often feel afraid to express support for the union, meaning that they could not possibly have a sense of how much support there was for a union without a "fair election" agreement.[34] José suggested that St. Joseph Health System loved immigrants, until they decide they want to form a union.

In 2007, 2008, and 2009, the system was given a Gallup Great Workplace Award by the Gallup polling organization. According to Gallup, the award "honors organizations for their commitment to providing a workplace that enables employees to be engaged and productive." It is based on surveys conducted among employees by the Gallup organization, which is paid consultancy fees. But while SJHS managers touted the award as a testament to its commitment to its employees, union supporters suggested that employees were not free to express their feelings openly. Dan remembered an intense competition among the managers of different departments in the hospital to achieve the highest Gallup scores. Managers told their employees that they "wanted to make the department look good," and they offered pizza parties to employees if they had the highest ratings in the hospital—an implicit bribe encouraging employees to give high scores. Some workers even reported managers looking over their shoulders while they filled out the surveys.

A Dignified Choice

A similar back-and-forth took place over the question of "freedom" to unionize. Although the theological argument between the union and the hospital administration often encompassed a larger debate over how best to create a workplace with "dignity," the narrower disagreement was over what constituted a free choice for workers.

The union realized that St. Joseph Health System had no *legal* obligation to go beyond the National Labor Relations Act, a point acknowledged by several religious leaders in the campaign. As Bishop Tod Brown of Orange County wrote in a public letter to workers and hospital management on May 9, 2008, "under civil law, Saint Joseph Healthcare System is within their rights to insist upon the procedures of the National Labor Relations Act." This sentiment was reflected by one local rabbi from whom the union was seeking support, who initially expressed reluctance to get involved: "I just don't believe, in my heart, that this is unjust. The Sisters are abiding by the law, right?"

In order to change the framework within which the election would take place, union leaders and workers had to take the campaign outside of the legal arena and out of the workplace, to the world of religious opinion and moral suasion. St. Joseph Health System may not have had a legal obligation to negotiate ground rules, but it did have a *moral* obligation, according to union supporters. In an editorial published in the *Santa Rosa Press Democrat*, Monsignor John Brenkle declared, "The structure created by the National Labor Relations Board is no longer a fair or adequate framework for moderating union organizing efforts."[35] Another local rabbi who supported the campaign quipped that Moses had not brought the NLRA down from the mountaintop. Behind such declarations was a belief that religious institutions must pay attention to *social rights* that exceed those rights recognized by labor law. These social rights were articulated most explicitly by Tom Schindler, a former priest who had spent more than twenty years as an ethicist for Mercy Health Services in Maryland, succeeding Jack Glaser there. Schindler had left Catholic healthcare in part because he saw it as having betrayed workers' right to organize,[36] and became one of the union's earliest religious supporters in Santa Rosa.

Schindler met with Santa Rosa Memorial Hospital workers in February 2006, but died suddenly in a swimming accident soon after this meeting. *National Catholic Reporter*, a prominent Catholic journal, published an article of his posthumously. He wrote, "Within the U.S. tradition . . . when it comes to a union campaign, each employee has a right to state his or her opinion and to vote for or against having a union. But so too does the hospital administration." This narrow attention to civil rights, however, obscured the fact that "an organization, including a hospital, has more power and resources" than a worker. Election ground rules would help to remedy this imbalance.

Union supporters also cited a working paper put out by the United States Council of Catholic Bishops in 1999, *A Fair and Just Workplace: Principles and Practices for Catholic Healthcare*. The document had been the result of discussions among a group of national labor leaders, hospital administrators, and bishops, who had begun to flesh out a framework for organizing in Catholic hospitals. It stated the desirability of election agreements like the one the union was advocating—thus distinguishing *moral* standards from legal standards. Having read the working paper, a local Catholic deacon expressed "concern" that the Sisters were "meeting the [standards] of the National Labor Relations Board, but not meeting the Bishops' standard."

The Sisters, and system executives, responded in writing that the union's interpretation of the working paper was wrong, and that "Catholic social teaching was about giving a voice to the voiceless." Granting one union an "exclusive agreement" regarding election ground rules would "shut out the individual voices of St. Joseph's workers at its individual hospitals." In interviews, St. Joseph Health System leaders expressed concern that the voices of *anti*union workers might be silenced. According to one Sister on the system's board, when a group of workers file for a union election, "to that group and to that position come a whole range of resources—money, training . . . the shirts and the buttons and all of that. And those resources are not available to the people who have a different opinion." For her, the field was lopsided in *favor* of the union. Another executive echoed this sentiment: "I think one of the things we struggle with a whole lot is that voice of the employee who may not want to be organized, who likes the working environment as they have it. Where's their voice?" For union supporters, the answer was obvious: all of management, implicitly and often explicitly, voiced its opposition to the union. The antiunion worker's "voice" had been projected loudly for years.

Theological Debate or Corporate Campaign?

The hospital leadership's most compelling response to the union's arguments, however, was that the union's attention to Catholic social teaching and the Sisters' legacy was itself merely instrumental, a "corporate campaign" intended to extort the hospital system and secure more dues-paying members. This argument had been developed by the U.S. Chamber of Commerce around the time of the Catholic Healthcare West campaign. The Chamber commissioned professor Jarol Manheim of George Washington University to write a report on union strategies. His brief, *Trends in Union Corporate Campaigns*, warned employers about what to expect from unions—from shareholder resolutions to conflict over theological teachings.[37] The intent of most such campaigns, Manheim implied, was to organize *employers* to recognize unions even without worker support.[38] In his earlier *The Death of a Thousand Cuts*, Manheim wrote that while the "core of the corporate campaign is a struggle for economic and/or political power, the public face of the campaign generally takes on the characteristics of a dramatic morality play in which the objective is to define and claim the moral high ground."[39] The symbolic dimension of these campaigns masked unions' underlying economic interests.

St. Joseph Health System ethicist Jack Glaser went further, telling union representatives that corporate campaigns were a form of "violence," which might be justified in extreme circumstances but were inappropriate within Catholic healthcare. Moreover, he wondered how the union could possibly expect to develop a productive relationship with Catholic hospitals after blemishing their reputations and undermining their work.[40] In a letter to Sisters in anticipation of union campaign activities, a Sister on the system's executive team argued, "Causing conflict and disunity are normative tactics of community organizers. . . . Our community's charism and mission is to bring unity and reconciliation—with God and neighbor. What they do is contrary to why we exist." In an e-mail message circulated to the press during the union's weeklong vigil in front of the Sisters' motherhouse in Orange, California, in July 2008, another Sister argued that the union's behavior was unethical because, rather than organize each hospital individually, the union had targeted the entire system.[41] In a private conversation between a prounion nun and Sister Katherine Gray, Gray expanded on this argument. The organizing drive, she said, was actually coming from the union, not from workers themselves. She claimed that SEIU had a national agenda to organize *all* healthcare workers, and that St. Joseph Health System was being targeted first for strategic reasons alone. An editorial in the *Orange County Register* put the point even more bluntly:

> This is really a story about power. There's fierce competition among unions to expand their membership in a declining economy and in a world where private-sector unionization is falling. One particular union, the Service Employees International Union United Healthcare Workers West, has crafted a plan to organize the entire St. Joseph system without having to go to the trouble of organizing each of the 14 hospitals that fall under that system.[42]

The entire St. Joseph Health System campaign was little more than a power grab, according to some, with SJHS a bit part in a larger play of the union's own making.

In response, union supporters argued that there was a distinction between a "corporate campaign" and a "comprehensive organizing campaign," the latter of which the union undertook unabashedly. What defined these sorts of campaigns, a union leader argued, was "working in coalitions to bring together workers, patients, community allies, and political leaders to advance a larger vision of the common good." And while this leader admitted to mobilizing allies in union campaigns, she argued that the union did so "to protect workers from what has become standard antiunion activity."[43] The theologian Joseph Fahey did not make the same distinctions, but equated the "corporate campaign" with "nonviolent campaigns that have been used throughout history including those waged by Gandhi, King, [and] Chavez." And while he recognized that it was preferable "to engage in persuasion rather than coercion," he argued that "coercion (of a nonviolent nature) is at times a necessity in securing justice."[44]

In order for its arguments to be effective, however, the union sought to support them through symbolic practices that gave the arguments moral legitimacy and showed the emotional authenticity of the union's relationship to Catholic teaching. Over the course of the Catholic campaign, the union subtly altered how it undertook protest and how it understood itself.

4

WINNING THE HEART WAY

Organizing and Cultural Struggle

When SEIU hired Eileen Purcell and Fred Ross Jr. to develop its Catholic strategy, the union gained tremendous credibility within the Catholic community. Ross and Purcell were widely recognized for their social justice work, and they had relationships with Catholic leaders across the state and country. Because of their prior work, Ross and Purcell knew and had worked alongside several of the Sisters of St. Joseph of Orange. Several Sisters of St. Joseph had been in contact with Ross during the farmworker movement in the 1970s; with Purcell during her tenure at the SHARE Foundation in the 1980s; and with both in support of citizenship and immigrant rights in the 1990s. Ross and Purcell not only brought understandings of multiple worlds to the union, but they brought new relationships to the union as well. And at the same time they pushed the Sisters of St. Joseph of Orange to change their perspectives on unions, they pushed the union to broaden its relationship with sisters. As a part of her work on Catholic healthcare, for example, Purcell began to attend a coalition of sisters working against human trafficking. Not only could Purcell deepen her relationships with the sisters through this work, but she could also demonstrate the common values the sisters and union shared regarding human rights and economic justice.

As the campaign shifted more fully into the religious arena, the union strategy was to encourage religious leaders—those seen as having moral legitimacy—to support the union's interpretation of Catholic social teaching, creating a crisis within the Catholic community that would propel the campaign toward settlement. This was no simple task. Religious leaders had good reasons not to want to get involved in a labor conflict, particularly one involving a religious institution. Many Catholic leaders had long-standing relationships with Sister Katherine Gray and other nuns in the Sisters of St. Joseph of Orange. Other prominent Catholic institutions relied on the Sisters for financial support. Moreover, religious leaders recognized the flexibility of theological argument and were skeptical of jumping into the fray of contentious politics. As one Santa Rosa monsignor told me, "Even the devil reads scripture," explaining that "scripture can be used for bad ends as well as good." Another priest whom I was trying to get involved in the campaign was even more direct: "You say one thing, the hospital says another thing. How do we know whom to believe?"

In my first meetings with religious leaders, I had little to go on beyond my limited powers of persuasion. I am not an especially religious person, but had the naïve vision of these leaders jumping at the chance to right a wrong within the faith community. After all, I thought, these religious leaders were insulated from business concerns and so would be able to see the Sisters' interpretation of Catholic teaching on labor as a cynical, market-driven morality. I quickly was disabused of these notions on a visit to Reverend Tom, a pastor and the president of the local Ministers' Prayer Fellowship Breakfast. After I finished describing the hospital's antiunion campaign, Reverend Tom expressed dismay that the Sisters were not doing God's will, were letting the market dictate the treatment of hospital workers. I felt as if he might jump at the chance to become involved.

But then Tom pointed to three pictures on his wall—one with Jesus leading sheep, one with Jesus comforting the sheep, and one with Jesus fighting wolves to protect the sheep. He discussed how an employer was responsible for leading employees, for comforting them, and for protecting them. He said his responsibility was to encourage employers to treat their workers well. As an example, he told a story about the workers doing construction in the back of his church. Several weeks before, Tom had gone to check on the work when he found the boss, a man Tom ministered to as part of a "business prayer fellowship," shouting at his employees. Tom took the employees aside and told them, "This guy, he was praying for you this morning. He really does care about you, but he's a young Christian so be patient with him." For Tom, a commitment to justice meant a commitment to encouraging beneficent employers, yet the employees were passive sheep needing to be led. After telling me that he would encourage his ministers' group to pray for a just resolution, our meeting was over. I had no luck deepening his engagement with the campaign.

Reverend Tom's paternalistic theological orientation, in hindsight, seemed almost impossible to reconcile with the argument the union sought to make. But his interpretation of Christian teaching seemed at least in part a product of his ongoing relationships with business owners in Santa Rosa, which implicitly framed the way he thought about workers' rights. Religious leaders were nested within existing social networks that influenced their openness to hearing about workers' desires for unionization. On my first visit to a Presbyterian minister, the minister's secretary flinched when I told her I was with SEIU. The minister would tell me later that the secretary's husband was a technical worker at the hospital who opposed the union. He said several congregants were doctors and managers at the hospital, and he expressed worry about the recent decline in the number of people who attended his congregation. So despite the rapport that I felt we developed over the course of a ninety-minute conversation, and despite his espoused desire to bring "issues of justice" to his congregation, I was not surprised when he stopped returning my phone calls.

When I visited a progressive Reform synagogue accompanied by the head of its social action committee, I was taken aback when the rabbi—having supported the Memorial organizing effort in the past—seemed to have cooled to the idea. He told me he could understand worker justice when it came to the farmworkers and other low-wage employees, but he said he did not understand why relatively well-paid hospital workers would need a union. I found out later that an administrator from another local hospital was on the board of the synagogue, and had chided the rabbi for his support of the Memorial campaign. A Lutheran minister's story was similar. At first his resistance to supporting the union seemed a theological one: he wanted to use social justice issues to unify his congregation rather than divide it, and he was worried that a union drive would deepen existing divisions among his flock. It was only toward the end of the conversation that he revealed he was close with someone at the hospital who had told him the union would disrupt the relationships between workers and management. Perhaps unsurprisingly, religious leaders were in some ways followers, their interpretations of doctrine influenced by those with whom they came into contact every day.

These preexisting relationships sometimes worked in the union's favor as well. An Episcopal priest knew a woman who had been a charge nurse at Memorial and had left her job because Memorial was "the most un-Christian place she had ever worked." He was also friends with an Episcopal chaplain who, according to the priest, had been fired from the hospital after giving last rites to a Roman Catholic when a Catholic priest was not available. A United Church of Christ minister had attended a mothers' group with a Latina hospital worker. And a couple of Latino workers on the organizing committee regularly attended local Catholic churches. José and his family were friends with the two priests at his local church. These relationships opened doors for the union that might otherwise have been closed.

Building Strategic Relationships

On the morning of Sunday, June 15, 2008, Monsignor John Brenkle of St. Helena Catholic Church celebrated the fiftieth anniversary of his ordination, and friends joined him from far and wide. Ross and Purcell were among these friends. Monsignor Brenkle traced his own political awakening to Bobby Kennedy. With a group of fellow seminarians, Brenkle had visited the Department of Justice in the midst of the civil rights movement. Kennedy, then the attorney general (and a Catholic), had addressed the group and challenged the Catholic Church to do more on behalf of the movement. It was with that in mind that Ross presented Brenkle with a framed collage that traced a social justice lineage from Kennedy, through Cesar Chavez and Dolores Huerta, to Brenkle himself, below the quote from Kennedy:

> Each time a person stands up for an ideal, or acts to improve the lot of others, or strikes out against injustice, he sends forth a tiny ripple of hope, and

crossing each other from a million different centers of energy and daring, these ripples build a current that can sweep down the mightiest walls of oppression and resistance.

Ross and Purcell had been introduced to Monsignor Brenkle in 2001 by Reverend Ray Decker, a lifelong friend, mentor, and colleague of Purcell's. Monsignor Brenkle was and remains one of the most highly respected religious leaders in Napa County, which is part of the Diocese of Santa Rosa that also includes Sonoma County. He is a trained canon lawyer and an ardent supporter of farmworker rights. He also has close relationships with growers, some of whom are members of his parish in St. Helena. He is a trusted adviser of the local bishop and once sat on a community outreach board at Queen of the Valley Hospital, a Napa hospital owned by St. Joseph Health System.

Brenkle had long had the respect of other priests in the diocese, and he became even more indispensable when several priests there were charged and convicted of sex-abuse crimes in the 1990s. The bishop at the time was charged with both abuse and embezzlement, having funneled diocesan contributions into payments to abuse victims and legal fees. By 2000 the diocese was in disgrace, and almost bankrupt. Brenkle not only served as financial officer for the diocese in the aftermath, but also chaired a review board to help rebuild congregants' faith in the church. A 2000 article in *Salon.com* reported on the process Brenkle helped lead:

> In the Diocese of Santa Rosa, leaders agreed to hold a series of town meetings, chaired by Brenkle, to let Catholic laymen as well as women, nuns and priests air their fear and anger. I attended one last month, and witnessed both the pain and the surprising healing power the scandals have unleashed within one corner of the church.[1]

By listening to the pain of abuse victims, Brenkle began a healing process that likely saved the diocese from bankruptcy. In the process he earned the eternal gratitude of the remaining diocesan leadership, and learned a thing or two about the Church's own moral failings.

Brenkle was also close to Sister Katherine Gray and others within the Sisters of St. Joseph of Orange. Sister Katherine had been a teacher at a Catholic school where Monsignor Brenkle had been principal, and Brenkle remembered her as "a talented woman," someone who "could come in to a meeting where there'd be all kinds of dissenting ideas and she would be able to synthesize and get people to focus on the central point." Another Sister was one of Brenkle's close friends, and had sewn a tapestry that hung on Brenkle's office wall.

Ross and Purcell started visiting St. Helena as early as 2001, anticipating that Brenkle might become an important ally, but he did not want to get involved. According to Brenkle, he "did not want to incur other people's anger or wrath." Purcell remembered, "He did not want to get involved initially because he had close ties with these Sisters." Brenkle was not alone. Those who had close ties with the Sisters were those least likely to get involved, but they also were the ones to whom the Sisters were most likely to listen. The costs to involvement were sometimes high. One former Sister of St. Joseph of Orange had stayed in touch with one of her mentors in the order, visiting her every week for many years. Yet when this former sister began to support the unionization effort, her mentor terminated all contact. One union leader discussed the situation with another sister whom she had known for decades: "She's shaking her head and you can tell she doesn't want to do anything about it. Because the St. Joseph Sisters have her come out there once a year to give a workshop, she doesn't want to sacrifice the relationship by holding them accountable." In the Catholic Healthcare West campaign, sisters throughout the country "closed ranks and were fiercely loyal to the Sisters' position." Some Sisters had even faced discipline or risked expulsion when they challenged system leaders.

Throughout the unionization effort at Santa Rosa Memorial Hospital, Purcell and Ross kept Brenkle informed about the campaign's ebb and flow, regularly driving the ninety minutes from Oakland to St. Helena. Monsignor Brenkle also became increasingly aware of St. Joseph Health System's antiunion stance during his involvement with Queen of the Valley Hospital. On one occasion in 2006, an SJHS ethicist appeared as a guest speaker at the hospital and began to attack the unionization drive. But it was Brenkle's ongoing relationships with Ross and Purcell that helped him have a change of heart.

Sociologists have shown the extent to which social networks can serve as resources for individuals, businesses, and social movement organizations.[2] Typically, however, networks are regarded as relatively static webs of relationships that precede and help to explain subsequent outcomes.

Community organizers in the union did not make use of existing social ties only, although these were certainly important. They also actively sought to establish and deepen relationships with key religious leaders who could provide symbolic legitimacy to the struggle. Relationships were discussed as things to be used strategically, "moral resources" that would increase rather than decrease if deployed, and might atrophy if underutilized.[3] At one point during the campaign, when I expressed a desire to return to my graduate studies, a leader of the campaign instructed me to begin to "decentralize my relationships," introducing others on the campaign to those with whom I was closest so that these allies could still be put to use by the union effort. Religious leaders got involved in the struggle not only because they believed it was the "right thing to do" but also because they were embedded within networks of relationships that the union fostered deliberately.

This is not to say that the relationships organizers developed on the campaign were fake or purely instrumental. Ross, Purcell, and other leaders on the campaign distanced themselves from organizers and organizations that treated religious leaders as interchangeable—"renting-a-collar" in organizing parlance. Ross and Purcell both emphasized the importance of ongoing relationships to the organizing effort. They each had longstanding relationships with faith leaders in California, and mined these relationships for connections to key actors who might have some influence with the Sisters of St. Joseph of Orange. In her summary of the St. Joseph Health System campaign, Purcell wrote:

> Strategic allies persevered and accompanied SJHS workers in part because of the long term relationships we established. Some engaged the fight because of long standing ties to Eileen and Fred. Others were recruited and cultivated with systematic outreach and follow-up. Our approach was relational, not transactional. The relationships were based on trust, shared vision, and honest, ongoing communication which earned credibility. They were dynamic and grew over time.[4]

Ross and Purcell were masters at developing relationships that were "not transactional" but at the same time helped build power on behalf of the union. According to Ross, both he and Eileen had "nurtured and developed lifelong relationships with people like Brenkle. So from the start, this is not going to end the day after the vote." Purcell recognized that "one of the great critiques of union organizers in the religious community is [that] we parachute in, we rent-a-collar, they come to the action, and that's it. That's not how we organize." For Purcell and Ross these relationships were long-term, reciprocal, and expansive—based on shared values more than narrow interests.

Nevertheless, despite this approach to relationships, there remained some tension in the union between the instrumental purposes for which relationships were established in the first place and the kind of emotional work necessary to sustain and develop these relationships. Said differently, if the instrumental nature of relationships was too obvious, the relationship was no longer useful. There is an element of exploration or of growth within relationships that cannot be reduced to exchange.

The tension between the instrumental and authentic was highlighted for me when I went to visit a Catholic priest with a Latina woman who worked at the hospital and attended the priest's church. Early on in our conversation the priest asked her, "Why should I give you my support?" The worker answered, "Because you baptized my children." Laughing, the priest responded, "That's not a good reason." Of course this connection *was* the reason union leaders thought the worker would be a good person to speak with the priest, but the extent to which the interaction was an exchange had to be couched in different terms. The priest demonstrated the implicit rules governing the exchange later in the same visit when the worker's friend—who was babysitting the worker's child outside while she spoke with the priest—asked the priest to bless her new house up in Santa Rosa and then asked how much the blessing cost. The priest responded, "Cost? It doesn't cost anything. You make a donation." The blessing was done for "free," with the donation a gift in return.

One priest whom I came to know through the campaign was supportive of workers' rights but skeptical about the union's strategy, criticizing it as being too instrumental. He said that he had a problem with all community organizers (failing to mention that I was having a conversation with him as a community organizer myself) because they were too "agentic," meaning their relationships were used for ends other than the relationship itself. He admitted that when he had been involved with community organizations in the past he "didn't have friendships that were just friendships." Rather, these friendships "had some other agenda attached—how they could help me with my projects." The priest seemed implicitly to be probing the extent to which *our* relationship was authentic or merely a result of my desire for his support. Organizers with the union overlooked these noninstrumental dimensions to relationships at their own peril.

A Unitarian minister admitted that our relationship was the reason he had gotten involved in the Memorial campaign. There are all sorts of injustices in the world to which he could usefully contribute his time, he told me. He admitted he had become involved in the Santa Rosa Memorial Hospital campaign because I was one of the people who showed up at the door to his church most consistently.

The union's relationships with religious leaders also put it in some tension with other faith-based community organizations in the area. The Industrial Areas Foundation (IAF)—an organization founded by Saul Alinsky that remains one of the most well-known progressive community organizing models in the country—had a fledgling chapter in the county and was in some ways a natural partner for the union. IAF organizers had relationships with important Catholic religious leaders in the area and were beginning to work more intensively with laity within these congregations as well. The union had staff members and financial resources that could help the IAF build its organization in the county and an interest in deepening its own involvement in the religious community.

In practice, however, an alliance was more difficult to strike on the ground.[5] The IAF model begins by having congregants deepen their relationships with one another through an extensive process of "one-on-ones" and "house meetings." One-on-ones are meetings between individuals in which people intentionally establish relationships with one another. House meetings are meetings organized by a leader in his or her own home, in which he or she invites a group of people to discuss some issue or deepen their relationships with one another. Through these different strategies of relationship building, IAF organizers help congregants identify common interests around which they can organize.[6] With the support of the IAF, one local Catholic church had recently spent over a year organizing the church's centennial celebration. The IAF organizer's theory was that organizing this celebration would give the congregation confidence to tackle an issue of broader public concern.

Although the union also believed in using one-on-ones and house meetings to deepen relationships, the union's issue—namely, workers' desire to form a union at Santa Rosa Memorial Hospital—was not up for negotiation. Although most union organizers shared an understanding of the importance of relationships to their work, the union had its own agenda and its own timeline. Moreover, union organizers tended to think that a clear goal enhanced the possibility of deepening relationships by providing a sense of urgency to people's work. The IAF criticized the union's desire to turn out religious leaders for public legitimacy without deep ties to the congregations of which the leaders were a part. The union tended to see the IAF as unfocused and unreliable, since IAF organizers refused to commit to particular "turnout" numbers for union events or to deliver specific, measurable results for the union.

At one point in the Memorial campaign, the union attempted to organize meetings within congregations, with the idea that these would build toward a large religious vigil several months later. The union thought that these meetings would inspire people to commit to turning out for the larger vigil. Those religious activists with IAF experience, however, thought this was disingenuous. One lay leader said that it "felt false," since house meetings—according to the IAF—were "only supposed to expand relationships, not get people to turn out to anything." At our "kickoff" meeting for the house meeting drive attended by fifteen or so religious leaders, a minister with the IAF facilitated. Beforehand, we had agreed that he would work to motivate the other leaders to have their own congregation meetings. In the middle of the meeting, however, he shifted course and allowed the meeting to end without anyone having committed to meetings within their congregations. In the end, union organizers and IAF organizers worked separately more often than they did together and occasionally—in moments that highlighted the absurdity of their failure to work together—would pass one another in church hallways for consecutive meetings with religious leaders.

Story Training and Workers' Symbolic Role

As the campaign shifted from the workplace to the community at large, workers came to play a more symbolic role. This is not to say that workers' cultural practices were insignificant as they recruited other workers to take part in the union effort initially, but rather that workers' capacities to represent themselves symbolically took on even more importance as the campaign moved to the religious arena.

Ross discussed the different philosophies within the union about how to run "fair election" campaigns. Some argued that since workers would not be voting until after an agreement was reached, organizing workers should not be a priority. He strongly disagreed. In order for the community campaign to be "authentic," he argued, the worker voice needed to be strong. The community at least needed to feel as though workers were leading the way. As Purcell wrote, "Workers' participation granted the campaign moral authority in the face of 'corporate campaign' charges and St. Joseph Health System management and sponsors' claims that workers did not want or need a union."[7]

This lesson was highlighted for Ross as he encouraged Monsignor Brenkle to become more involved in the campaign. Brenkle had been reluctant to get involved in the campaign because, according to Fred, he "had been friends for thirty-five years with some of the leaders inside St. Joseph's and he didn't want to risk that friendship." Yet in early 2006, as the union began to campaign for election ground rules, the CEO of St. Joseph Health System, Deborah Proctor, asked to set up a meeting with Brenkle, the diocese's bishop, Santa Rosa Memorial's CEO George Perez, and the system's theologian. The bishop, still reeling from the diocese's recent sex scandal, told the three SJHS executives, "What I don't need is another controversy. I want to see this settled quietly and out of the public." Brenkle remembered Perez responding, "Well, bishop, it's not a problem because I can't think of more than twenty people who would even care about a union." Unbeknownst to the executives, however, Ross had armed Brenkle with a petition recently signed by eighty-seven union supporters (which the union had also sent to Perez). Brenkle asked Perez, "Do these eighty-seven people work for you?" and left the meeting thinking the hospital leaders "[didn't] know [their] people."

In this meeting with St. Joseph Health System leadership, Brenkle was also led to believe that the system would negotiate election ground rules if a new majority of workers at Memorial expressed interest in organizing. Although Ross was skeptical, he knew that "Brenkle [was] ready to go to the mat on this, and he [could] bring the bishop along." As worker leaders began collecting their co-workers' signatures again, according to Ross, Brenkle became more invested in the campaign, "would want to get updated on a weekly basis," and "began to get creative." Brenkle became a powerful ally because the union demonstrated workers' support: "We'd have no credibility if the workers had not gone out and gotten a new majority."

I learned about the importance of worker stories the hard way during my first religious "support committee" meeting. I had assumed that workers needed to focus on their workplace, and so I made little effort to ensure a good worker presence at the meeting. By the time the meeting started, there were fifteen religious leaders and no workers. José, a young Latino immigrant and kitchen worker at the hospital, arrived late and froze when invited to speak, having never spoken before a large group before, let alone a gathering of religious leaders. Nevertheless, I thought the meeting had gone well, and was surprised to get a call a few days later from a Catholic priest who "hadn't cared for it." When I probed, he continued, "Well, it's just a bunch of liberal progressive people who are trying to strategize for the workers, so I'm going to withdraw my hat until I feel like this is something that workers want."

Workers' stories and experiences were critical for generating support within the broader community. Although several scholars of social movements have highlighted the importance of storytelling or narrative to movement success, few have examined the ways that social movement actors learn to tell their stories—through an educative process.[8] Organizers spent a great deal of time coaching workers about how to tell these stories persuasively, and institutionalizing worker stories in order to pass them on to allies. As I was preparing to bring a worker to meet with a religious leader, an organizer instructed me to make sure the worker told a particular story—one in which a supervisor told her that the union "wanted to sink their fangs" into the hospital. The organizer was worried that the priest might not understand the worker's Spanish accent, however, and so wanted me to "make sure [the priest] hears the 'fang' part." During another event, the union's videographer stood directly in front of a speaker while she began crying as she recounted the intimidation she felt from managers. An organizer told me that she thought the event lost its "authenticity" when it seemed like a "photo opportunity" for the videographer—that the drama on camera came at the expense of people's experiences at the event.

From one perspective, it is easy to see the process of story training as manipulative. But, as a union leader pointed out, most people "get paralyzed when you deal with power." Even more generally, most people do not have experience telling their personal stories in a public way. Only a year or so after José had frozen at my religious support committee meeting, he had become a powerful voice on behalf of the union as a result of working with union organizers—testifying at a congressional roundtable on the need for labor law reform, speaking in front of hundreds at rallies, and defending himself and co-workers in meetings with supervisors. On several occasions, before workers met with system leaders, union leaders would role-play the meetings so that workers could practice "claiming [their] story." Like anything else, articulating one's experiences and communicating one's emotions take practice.

Workers' stories served both affective and cognitive purposes. Emotionally, the stories "humanized the conflict and its impact on workers and their families," as Purcell put it. Yet the stories were also carefully documented and organized as evidence to prove the union's "case" to the public. Although the hospital argued on multiple occasions that the antiunion conduct was the work of isolated "bad apple" managers, the union's compilation of stories revealed an indisputable pattern of antiunion behavior. A website run by the union contained an updated chronology of the system's antiunion conduct, including "specific references to NLRB ULP [unfair labor practice] findings, anti-union power points, and worker and allies' testimony."[9]

If the deliberate production and documentation of stories made them slightly less spontaneous, the institutionalization of stories was essential to workers' new role in the campaign. Workers' capacity to motivate religious leaders to action rested as much on their capacities for storytelling as on their aggregate numbers. And while the most powerful stories were told in the context of relationships, the union could reach a national audience through the collection and dispersal of the hospital's most egregious behaviors. In the fall of 2005 and again in the fall of 2007, the union produced reports that featured individual workers' stories—their reasons for wanting a union, and the hospital's concerted attempts to stop them. In the second report the union enclosed a DVD compilation of workers' stories and allies' arguments.

Enactment: Putting Union Theology into Practice

The union also explicitly framed its events as part of a coherent narrative, choosing dates for events that would help tie the struggle to historical victories. After the Orange County blitz in February 2007, for example, the union held its founding organizing committee meeting in Orange on Cesar Chavez's birthday, March 31. In her summary of the campaign, Eileen Purcell discussed how the union "consciously reinforced our message by careful choice of symbols."[10] The symbol of a peace dove, used on posters and cards in preparation for one "procession" in the fall of 2007, was "an explicit effort to lift up hope for reconciliation."[11] The slogan, "Our Values, Our Voice, Our Choice," was intended "to emphasize workers' pride in SJHS as an institution and their commitment to the shared values of 'dignity, excellence, service, and justice.'"[12] The climax of the campaign—a weeklong vigil outside the Sisters' motherhouse in July 2008—coincided with the thirty-fifth anniversary of the United Farm Workers' strike in Fresno, California, during which several Sisters of St. Joseph of Orange went to jail with striking farmworkers.

The union's rhetorical and symbolic strategies were debated and discussed intensely among union leadership, but they could not be carried out without the consent of lower-level organizers and worker leaders. At one point two veterans of the United Farm Workers, Reverend Chris Hartmire and Jerry Cohen, took center stage. Chris Hartmire was a Presbyterian minister who had spent more than twenty-five years leading the National Farm Worker Ministry in support of the UFW. In 1999, Hartmire had also led the Sacramento Fair Election Committee during the CHW elections. Jerry Cohen had been chief counsel for the UFW and later for Neighbor-2-Neighbor. Both were close friends of Fred Ross. Together, Hartmire and Cohen fleshed out an idea that workers participate in a fast to win a fair election agreement from the Sisters. Over the course of a weekend retreat, they described the historical roots of the fast and distinguished a "fast" from a "hunger strike."[13] During their presentation, they argued that a fast was expressive—a moral act—whereas a "hunger strike" was instrumental, intended merely to accomplish an objective. Yet the distinction seemed lost on the younger staff, who continued to question the "authenticity" of a fast given that we *did*, in fact, want to convince St. Joseph Health System to change its practices. Workers had doubts about the fast as well. Brandon recalled that workers "thought it was a terrible idea. . . . Most people were like, 'That's crazy, we're not going to do that.'" A weeklong vigil took the place of the fast.

What to call the campaign's *goal* was up for debate as well. Organizers in Santa Rosa had expressed concern that the term "fair election agreement" sounded as if it referred only to the *day* of the election, whereas the union was most concerned about the period leading up to the election. During one meeting at union headquarters, several members of the union's communications staff helped brainstorm a new phrase. "Fair election campaign" had been the phrase of choice among several organizers, but it was rejected by the organizing director who felt that use of the word "campaign" might legitimize the hospital running an *anti*union campaign. "We don't really want them to be able to campaign," he said. A member of the communications staff wondered aloud whether any polling had been done on the phrase that resonated most with workers. And while "free and fair election" had polled best in Ohio, it was unclear whether the same would be true for workers at Santa Rosa Memorial Hospital. Unable to come to a conclusion during that meeting, we continued to use "fair election agreement" in most of our literature.

Finally, the union struggled with how to refer to the Sisters' failure to abide by Catholic social teaching. It was Monsignor Brenkle who came up with the term on which the union would settle: "disconnect." As a union leader explained to me, "I thought it was just one of the most brilliant things I've ever learned about how to call somebody out as being a hypocrite without using the term 'hypocrite.' The 'disconnect' means you can connect it ... and that's why it's so brilliant. I guess it takes seventy-five years to learn certain things." Another organizer explained in slightly different terms how calling on the Sisters to live up to their values would make it easier for the union to achieve its goals:

> In a campaign like this where you're trying to force an institution to do something they don't want to do, if they claim to have values and you can put what you want them to do in terms of their values, it's an out for them. They can be like, "We're going to follow our values and do the right thing." Rather than, "We're just going to capitulate to this organization that's been trashing us for the last couple of years."

The union would be disciplined about how it spoke about the campaign, framing it in such a way as to make reconciliation possible. Not only would this give hospital leaders a face-saving way of conceding to the union, but it would also leave open the possibility of a working partnership in the future.

Turning Texts into Tools

One union leader described the campaign within the religious community as a process of "information organizing," or making the union's own interpretation of Catholic social teaching increasingly legitimate within the religious community as a whole. The significance of this teaching to labor organizing in Catholic healthcare was exemplified by the formation, in 1998, of a "subcommittee on Catholic Healthcare" within the United States Conference of Catholic Bishops (USCCB) that included national labor leaders, hospital administrators, and bishops. The committee's purpose was to make recommendations for Catholic hospital systems facing unionization drives. The committee's formation had been requested by Sister Mary Roch Rocklage, president and CEO of the Sisters of Mercy Health System in St. Louis, in the midst of the contentious Catholic Healthcare West campaign.[14] Over the course of the next year, the committee would hold a series of meetings. The result, issued in May 1999, was a "working paper" entitled *A Fair and Just Workplace: Principles and Practices for Catholic Healthcare*. The document clearly stated the value of unions as reflected in Catholic social teaching and recommended the adoption of ground rules at the front end of organizing drives like those the union was advocating.

The working paper quickly became a focus of attention among Catholic health systems and labor unions. It was debated in formal hearings sponsored by Catholic dioceses, and received national media attention.[15] Labor unions tended to consider the working paper a victory, despite their recognition that it was a "compromise document," and did not include language supportive of employer "neutrality," or of "card check" elections—a process by which workers are able to unionize without a vote if a majority sign cards. Healthcare administrators and sisters involved in Catholic hospitals, however, repudiated the document, alleging that the working paper misinterpreted Catholic social teaching and that it failed to outline mechanisms that would hold labor unions accountable for their actions. Nevertheless, in April 2001 the working paper became a model for the election process agreed to by SEIU and Catholic Healthcare West. It seemed to many in organized labor that a new model might be on the horizon.[16]

But despite the "partnership" between SEIU and CHW, and despite ongoing work by the USCCB subcommittee, the working paper remained a source of contention in the St. Joseph Health System campaign. In 2005, at the suggestion of Monsignor Brenkle, the union had "published" the working paper as an official-looking pamphlet, which it distributed widely to Catholic leaders and community supporters in an effort to put pressure on St. Joseph Health System. The system responded by working to undermine the document's importance. In 2006, Sister Katherine Gray and CEO Deborah Proctor traveled to Spokane, Washington, to meet with Bishop William Skylstad, the national chair of the Conference of Catholic Bishops at the time the working paper was written. Upon return, they reported that the guidelines were not official policy of the council, and that—in fact—not a single diocese in the country had ratified them.

In response, Ross and Purcell suggested to Monsignor Brenkle that Santa Rosa become the first diocese in the country to formalize the working paper as official diocesan policy. And so with Monsignor Brenkle's blessing, in January 2007 Ross and Purcell attended a meeting of the Santa Rosa Diocese's Priests' Council and presented the council with a proposal to adopt the working paper. Unfortunately, Monsignor Brenkle was unable to attend the meeting, which meant that the union's biggest advocate in the diocese was unable to speak on the union's behalf. Ross and Purcell were also caught by surprise when a priest whom they did not know spoke up in the meeting to say that the conflict was "not any of the diocese's business." It turned out that this priest had a biological sister who was a Sister of St. Joseph of Orange. The priest's intervention put the proposal on hold, as the Council decided to invite representatives from St. Joseph Health System to give their perspective. Still, after three representatives from SJHS came to speak at the next month's council, the diocese voted 11–1 to adopt the working paper. In an op-ed by Brenkle published on May 11, 2007, he announced, "The Santa Rosa Diocesan Priests' Council voted in favor of [the working paper's] adoption in March, and Bishop Walsh confirmed that recommendation. The diocese is committed to using these guidelines, and we encourage St. Joseph Health System to follow suit."[17] Within the next few months the diocese would begin discussions with union organizers and thirteen of its cemetery workers about ground rules for a union election; educators in the diocese's Catholic schools were also promised the same. St. Joseph Health System did not follow suit, however.

Between 2004 and 2005, as the St. Joseph Health System campaign began, Catholic hospital organizing campaigns were intensifying in Ohio, Illinois, Oregon, and New York. As tensions mounted and the conflicts between Catholic hospital employers and unions continued, a meeting was set for the bishops' subcommittee in June 2006. In the meantime, the CHA's newly appointed president, Daughter of Charity sister Carol Keehan, agreed to allow SEIU to attend the annual CHA convention in Orlando, Florida, which was meeting the week before the scheduled subcommittee. Workers from St. Joseph Health System and other systems joined several union leaders at the convention. During this convention, for the first time, Sister Katherine and Deborah Proctor met with workers from Santa Rosa Memorial Hospital. But despite this small breakthrough, the CHA meeting also revealed the depth of the mistrust between labor and the Catholic healthcare industry. One of the Memorial workers was threatened with arrest for passing out a written appeal for dialogue to bridge the divide and join together in a common cause, after CHA staff reported that SEIU was irreverently leafleting the plenary. As a result, Sister Keehan broke off all contact with SEIU and the USCCB subcommittee. The subcommittee meeting was postponed.

It was not until 2007 that the bishops' subcommittee reconvened, with several bishops, labor representatives, and sisters and hospital administrators from those systems (including SJHS) that were enmeshed in labor organizing struggles. Yet in the fall of 2007, the CEO of St. Joseph Health System, Deborah Proctor, withdrew from the national table, citing the union's "corporate campaign" against the system. Her withdrawal was in direct violation of a commitment among all parties to refrain from bringing local conflicts to the national table. Within the St. Joseph Health System campaign, hopes for a settlement at the national level waned.

Building legitimacy within the religious community also involved appeals to recognized Catholic scholars who might support the union's perspective. Joseph Fahey became one of the most important of these scholars. A professor of religious studies at Manhattan College, Fahey had recently helped organize Catholic support for workers seeing to unionize with AFSCME at Chicago's Resurrection Hospital System. In the aftermath of this effort, Fahey began working with other Catholic scholars to found a national group, Catholic Scholars for Worker Justice.

As Fahey launched this initiative, in January 2008, Purcell invited Fahey to meet with workers at St. Joseph Health System. During his visit to California he also met with SJHS ethicists Jack Glaser and Kevin Murphy. His visit coincided with a vigil outside Santa Rosa Memorial Hospital, at which he spoke on the rights of workers to organize. The next day the *San Francisco Chronicle* printed an article on the vigil and a photo of Fahey above a caption that described him "fir[ing] up the crowd."[18] A testy back-and-forth ensued between Glaser and Fahey. Glaser wrote an e-mail to Fahey in which he admitted feeling betrayed, since Fahey had not disclosed that his trip was arranged in large part by the union. Fahey wrote back to say that he had no obligation to disclose his other activities during his visit. Each implicitly questioned the objectivity of the other, suggesting that the other's theological position was a result of their more secular interests. Fahey would return from California even more determined to build a coalition of like-minded scholars. Within a year he had organized a group of approximately two hundred scholars.

Going Public

As the prospects for establishing ground rules on the national level dimmed, the union sought to amplify the theological debate as widely as possible to maximize pressure on the Sisters. In February 2007, in Santa Rosa, the union organized a full-page ad supporting the union signed by local religious leaders and laypeople that was printed in the *Santa Rosa Press Democrat*. Sister Katherine Gray personally called each of the Catholic priests who had signed the advertisement to explain her position—which the union took to mean that it was doing something right.

The union's media strategy was made up of both "earned" and "paid" media coverage—"earned" meaning stories written about the union, and "paid" meaning advertisements bought by the union. Union leaders thought of their media strategy as a mini campaign. When the main local paper, the *Santa Rosa Press Democrat*, failed to cover a well-attended congressional hearing on the Memorial campaign that the union had organized in May 2007, for example, a union leader called the paper to seek recompense. The paper offered to publish an op-ed by Monsignor Brenkle in which he announced the diocese's adoption of the U.S. Conference of Catholic Bishops organizing guidelines. In Southern California, the union broke into the Spanish language media with stories of Latino worker leaders who had been threatened by managers as a result of their activism.

Over the course of the next two years, calls for election ground rules by prominent religious and community leaders mounted. In August 2007 the union produced an extensive report and DVD that exposed the system's antiunion activities in both Santa Rosa and Orange County, highlighted the Santa Rosa Diocese's adoption of the Council of Catholic Bishops guidelines, and suggested the need for "fair election" ground rules. The union sent the pamphlet to national Catholic, Protestant, and Jewish leaders. In response, St. Joseph Health System published full-page advertisements in eight California newspapers, and sent DVDs of their own to twenty-one thousand of their hospital workers that praised SJHS and congratulated workers for the system's recent Gallup Great Workplace Award.

On September 20, 2007, the National Coalition of American Nuns (NCAN), one of the more progressive coalitions of nuns in the country, issued a statement supportive of workers' organizing efforts. On October 19, the renowned theologian Rosemary Radford Ruether published a piece in the *National Catholic Reporter* reporting on both sides of the struggle within St. Joseph Health System.[19] Some union leaders seemed to think that Ruether's article was weak, leaving the reader with a feeling of "he said, she said," but the article had an impact nonetheless—the union would later learn that the Sisters and SJHS leadership were "devastated" by it.[20] Alongside these opinion pieces, Orange County media started paying attention to the campaign as well. In August 2007, coinciding with the release of the union's report, the *OC Weekly* (Orange County Weekly) began a series that would culminate in a front-page story about the campaign that November.[21] The more conservative *Orange County Register* began covering the campaign as well.[22]

The campaign reached a crescendo in July 2008 with a weeklong vigil in front of the Sisters' motherhouse during the Sisters' annual gathering. Encouraged by the union's media staff, reporters from the *New York Times*, the *Los Angeles Times*, and National Public Radio all covered the event. As Ross recalled, at the beginning of the vigil, workers had asked the Sisters for a meeting but were told that the Sisters were deep in prayer and reflection and so were unable to meet. But then a reporter from the *New York Times* came out for a day "and all of a sudden [Sister Kit] is able to come out of prayer and reflection and meet with him and the CEO and [the human relations director]." The *L.A. Times* was given the same access. For one union leader, the picture of the St. Joseph Health System leadership in the *L.A. Times* was "worth the price of gold." For the first time, they seemed "stern and angry and before that they'd always had this phony façade." Much of the media coverage discussed the conflict from the perspective of both labor and management. But even more important than the content of the coverage, for many union leaders, was the fact that they had successfully broadened the scope of conflict, and made the campaign at St. Joseph Health System a national story.

Throughout the campaign there had been signs that St. Joseph Health System was feeling the pressure. In late 2006, as the "fair election" campaign began to escalate, SJHS issued a unilateral "Code of Conduct for Third Party Representation Discussions." This document outlined the steps it would take to ensure a fair election, short of negotiating with the union. In the code of conduct the system committed itself to providing "factual" and "honest" information to employees, and promised it would not "hold mandatory meetings for the sole purpose of discussing our views on third-party representation."[23] As the campaign heated up in 2007 and 2008, the system went further, pledging not to use "union avoidance law firms," and promising not to use one-on-one meetings instigated by supervisors to discourage unionization. Nevertheless, the system consistently refused to negotiate such ground rules with the union; refused to outline steps it would take to provide union organizers and prounion worker leaders access to workers; would not discuss any process by which public materials might be reviewed by the other side; and—most important—refused any sort of outside or third-party enforcement of their commitments.

And then finally there was a breakthrough. On July 15, 2008, Catholic Scholars for Worker Justice issued a public statement to Sister Katherine Gray calling on St. Joseph Health System to negotiate election ground rules. In August, Sister Katherine responded to the scholars and for the first time expressed a willingness to negotiate ground rules once 30 percent of eligible workers had expressed interest in unionization—not only at Santa Rosa Memorial Hospital, but at any SJHS hospital. As union leaders and SJHS executives prepared to sit down at the negotiating table, the union kept the pressure on, paying for a series of four advertisements in the *National Catholic Reporter* in the summer and fall of 2008. For Labor Day, Sister Amata Miller, an economist and former board member of Catholic Health Initiatives, one of the largest Catholic health systems in the country, published an article in *America*, a weekly Jesuit magazine, entitled "Organizing Principles: Why Unions Still Matter." It seemed that a settlement was within reach.

Getting the Message

For union leaders, the system's agreement to negotiate "fair election" ground rules was powerful evidence of the campaign's success. As recently as June 2008, when four California bishops had sent a letter to St. Joseph Health System leaders urging them to negotiate, the system had refused. But by August, after national press coverage and growing attention within the Catholic Church, the system had agreed.

Nevertheless, system leaders claimed their changing position was not a concession to union pressure but was part of an ongoing process of "discernment." One system executive explained, "I honestly believe the reason we got to the point was we had dialogue and we learned a whole lot more about each other." He suggested that because he and union leaders were able to talk "as people," instead of "shouting from buildings five miles apart," union leaders and system executives were able to find common ground. When I responded that the change in the system's position seemed to correspond with the crescendo of the union's campaign, he demurred: "We didn't respond to that because it's not in our tradition to do that. But we also had dialogue during that period of time. . . . Not that we were forced because of this campaign, because we were stalwart in that campaign, and we were going to continue with our values regardless." According to another executive, the Sisters' charism—which he termed the values "they hold themselves accountable" to—is "unity and reconciliation." Because of this orientation, the system "cannot live its charism without being in dialogue with people constantly about this, and trying to move us to places where we have some reconciliation, where we have some unity. And that's really been our goal all the way through this." One ethicist for the system suggested that "this pounding adversarial [relationship] really doesn't get us where we need to get to."

Perhaps it is not surprising that SJHS executives denied conceding to external pressure even if—in November 2008—they made the cessation of public advertisements and public actions a condition of negotiating ground rules. Nevertheless, it would be simplistic to argue that SJHS executives were merely dishonest in their account of their internal process. Indeed, throughout the campaign they had been willing to dialogue with union leaders and other interested parties. Of course it would be equally simplistic to accept SJHS executives' account of their "discernment" as taking place within a neutral space of dialogue and self-reflection, a space free from power relations. It was no coincidence that their discernment led to negotiations with the union only *after* the union had brought the system's contradictory position on Catholic social teaching to national attention. Union leaders pointed out that the willingness of St. Joseph Health System to dialogue always seemed a result of pressure. At those moments in the campaign when the union was not putting pressure on the system, the system's willingness to dialogue seemed to evaporate.

St. Joseph Health System was not made economically or politically vulnerable by the union's campaign; the system did not concede based on a narrow conception of the corporation's interests. For the leaders of the system, however, who considered themselves the stewards of the legacy of the Sisters of St. Joseph of Orange, the contradiction between this legacy and their antiunion practices had become untenable.

But despite the union's success at winning negotiations, there were other more ominous messages lurking in its aftermath. When the *New York Times* covered the St. Joseph Health System campaign in July 2008 it was the first time in a decade that an SEIU healthcare organizing campaign had gotten such prominent coverage. But when Ross and Purcell sent a report about the press coverage to the international union, they did not get so much as a phone call in response. By the end of 2008, Ross and Purcell argued, the St. Joseph Health System campaign was the only existing religious healthcare campaign in the country that held any promise.[24] But aside from Ross and Purcell, who were still officially on the staff of the international union, the international remained uninterested in the breakthrough. In fact, behind the scenes, it appeared that the international was working to *prevent* the local's success. In the next chapter I explore the internal divisions within the labor movement that jeopardized workers' chances to win their union at Santa Rosa Memorial Hospital.

TROUBLE IN THE HOUSE OF LABOR

Alternative Visions of New Unionism

The union's cultural strategy in the St. Joseph Health System campaign relied on a rare collaboration between the international office of SEIU and the United Healthcare Workers West (SEIU-UHW) local. At the national level, union representatives forged a common language and common ideology with Catholic hospital representatives that manifested itself in the publication of the working paper *A Fair and Just Workplace* in 1999. In 2009 this position was formalized with the publication of *Respecting the Just Rights of Workers: Guidance and Options for Catholic Health Care and Unions*. In this national conversation union and Catholic hospital leaders recognized that they had much in common, from a concern for the uninsured to an interest in an overhaul of the healthcare system. And at an abstract level, they agreed on principles that should guide union organizing and union representation in Catholic hospitals.

At the local level, the St. Joseph Health System campaign ensured that national negotiations occurred from a position of strength rather than weakness, grounding the national roundtable's abstract principles in concrete gains for workers. Without the national roundtable, SJHS would have been under less pressure to frame its position in relationship to Catholic social teaching. Without local contestation, they would have had less incentive to get to national agreement, and no accountability to the common principles agreed upon at the national roundtable. Perhaps most important of all, the stories and experiences of St. Joseph Health System workers helped the national union's broader theological arguments resonate.

Ross and Purcell were bridges between the local and the international. Although officially on the staff of the international union, they worked intensely on the St. Joseph Health System campaign. Ross led the SJHS campaign with the SEIU-UHW organizing director, Glenn Goldstein. Eileen split her time between St. Joseph Health System and other national Catholic hospital campaigns. Together, Ross and Purcell helped to bridge the philosophical and strategic differences between the international and local, by helping the local to see the importance of the national discussions, and by helping the international to see the importance of local struggle. And for both the local and the international, the strategy at SJHS required something of a leap of faith. According to Eileen, "Ordinarily a union wouldn't invest these kinds of resources in a multiyear relationship-oriented organizing campaign." But between 2006 and 2009 the local and the international had worked together, and the work was finally beginning to pay off. With the local's commitment to workers and the international's broader resources and relationships, the campaign was able to "shine the spotlight on injustice," as Ross described it, "lifting up the disconnect, the contradictions."

At the very moment of greatest hope for the St. Joseph Health System campaign, however, the partnership between the international and the local collapsed. There had always been tensions between the organizations, differences in philosophy that were exacerbated by differences in the personalities of the organizations' charismatic leaders, SEIU president Andy Stern and United Healthcare Workers West president Sal Rosselli. But on the morning of January 27, 2009, the international union put the local in trusteeship, firing its leadership. Within a week, almost all local staff members would be terminated; the locks on UHW headquarters would be changed; and the struggle to organize Santa Rosa Memorial Hospital would again be postponed. Ross and Purcell would leave SEIU later that same year. Even if workers *could* have gone ahead with an election at

228Chapter 5

Memorial, SJHS's primary critique of unions in general—that they were adversarial organizations more concerned with their own perpetuation than with the workers they purported to serve—had a new Exhibit A. If the Sisters of St. Joseph of Orange were unaccountable to their workers, could any union do better?

In this chapter, I examine the conflict between UHW and the international union. Practically, I explore how the trusteeship undermined the St. Joseph Health System campaign, yet simultaneously provided new opportunities for growth and leadership among workers in Santa Rosa. Theoretically, I explore the different visions of unionism represented by the two sides in the conflict, visions that map onto an ongoing debate within labor scholarship between "top-down" and "bottom-up" unionism. For the local union, the international leadership was seen as a cadre of corrupt elites who sacrificed members' well-being for their own economic and political ends. For the international, local leaders were obstructionist, parochial renegades, manipulating and swindling their members while interfering with the national program.

Yet beneath the vitriol, real questions for the labor movement surfaced. The polarization between the local and the international overshadowed what was in fact a healthy debate about the purposes and possibilities of labor unions—one that runs deeper than the rhetoric of either side. In this chapter, moreover, I suggest that the two visions represented in the conflict were not mutually exclusive; indeed, a successful labor movement likely requires their convergence.

Collateral Damage

SEIU's international office in Oakland was on the seventh floor of a high-rise near the Oakland Airport. On the wall by the front doors of the office, framed portraits of Andy Stern, Mary Kay Henry, and other international executives formed a pyramid. From the large windows in the meeting room one could make out the Port of Oakland and, in the distance, downtown Oakland. But the most noticeable feature of the office was its silence. I had grown accustomed to the chaos of the local, where the parking lot was always overflowing and the hum of conversation inescapable. At the international office almost no one was ever around.

On Monday, January 26, 2009, the international office was even quieter than usual. International staff, whose ranks were swollen with reinforcements from around the country, had taken up residence at larger offices in nearby Alameda to plan the takeover, or trusteeship, of the local, United Healthcare Workers West. Many of those at the local, meanwhile, were camping out day and night in their headquarters to stave off international intruders. Behind closed doors, Ross and Purcell led a small meeting to discuss whether it would be possible to continue the St. Joseph Health System campaign in the face of the trusteeship. The meeting was a UFW reunion of sorts—Ross and Purcell had invited Chris Hartmire to attend and Jerry Cohen called in by phone. The UFW alumni gave the meeting a certain poignancy. The gathered group all remembered the purges and estrangement that debilitated the UFW from within.[1] So much had been lost from internecine wrangling. And so much was now at stake. International staff had suggested to Ross and Purcell that the St. Joseph campaign might be "collateral damage," a painful but necessary price for getting the local back under control. And despite attempts by many to orchestrate some sort of reconciliation, the leaders on each side seemed to be digging in their heels for a fight. Both the local and international had been orchestrating events to shore up support. Turning people out, Cohen remarked, was how you show "God is on your side." But what were these different conceptions of unionism anyway?

Growing Pains

For SEIU's international leadership, the possibilities for working-class power rested on the union's capacity to centralize authority and become a political force. One international staff person explained that since "wealth and decision-making is more centralized" among corporations, in turn labor had to "get more centralized. The employer picture is going to fashion the labor picture in response." Even more controversially, Andy Stern had made growth *the* central priority for the union: "The theory is the bigger we are, the more strength we have to [enact] public policy and hold to account employers who have gotten bigger and more centralized." For the international leadership, "When you do the power analysis, the way to preserve the gains and advance . . . requires exponential growth, and the way you get exponential growth is you look at all options, and that's what Andy was willing to do when no one else was willing to do it." By this logic, the union's responsibility for its members necessitated "maximum flexibility and . . . realpolitik." A local union's narrow focus on its own membership—rather than on members across the country or on the *unorganized*—meant, according to the international, that a local would never voluntarily take the risks or make the compromises necessary on behalf of the working class as a whole.

Underlying Stern's commitment to growth and centralized authority was a pragmatic political philosophy resonant with—if distinct from—Adam Przeworski's analysis of socialist political parties in his *Capitalism and Social Democracy*.[2] Przeworski discusses how the decision by socialist parties to enter electoral politics in the early twentieth century effectively made it impossible for such parties to base themselves solely in a self-identified "working class." Since a working class could never become a majority of voters in society, a socialist party was left with a choice between being "a party homogenous in its class appeal but sentenced to perpetual electoral defeats and a party that struggles for electoral success at the cost of diluting its class character."[3]

For Przeworski, working-class parties became diluted because they were compelled to appeal to the middle classes. Stern and SEIU, however, tended to reach out not to the middle class but to capital itself. Winning a voice for workers demanded that the union sometimes work in *partnership* with business. Oftentimes this meant that the union had to make significant compromises—for example, gaining organizing rights in exchange for the union's political advocacy on behalf of a company or concessions by the company's organized workforce. During contract negotiations with the Tenet Healthcare Corporation in 2006, the international made a deal that gave the union bargaining rights at twenty-three additional Tenet hospitals nationwide but made concessions on behalf of organized hospital workers in California (the concessions were later withdrawn, after outrage from UHW).[4]

The paradox for Przeworski was that "class shapes political behavior of individuals only as long as people who are workers are organized politically as workers."[5] As socialist parties built bridges with other social groups in order to gain political power, workers' identities *as workers* diminished. Stern's desire for SEIU to become a political power on behalf of the working class, paradoxically, made less clear what it meant to be a member of the working class at all.

At the micro level, Stern's philosophy of centralization and political compromise meant that worker political education often was given short shrift. A local organizer remembered hearing from the international, "Listen, don't go into workplaces talking about class. Don't go into workplaces talking about distribution of wealth. Don't go in talking about those things because workers don't care about that, that's not where workers are at." And while this organizer agreed that "there's some validity to how you frame those conversations [and] you don't go in with the *Communist Manifesto*," he continued, "eventually, you have to get to the conversation with homecare workers, 'Why are you getting paid $10 an hour?'"

Workers sometimes were left out of the equation altogether. When developing the union's Catholic healthcare strategy, one international leader recalled, the assembled group formulated criteria in order to prioritize organizing in different systems. She remembered suggesting, "'Shouldn't the number-one criterion be worker interest?' And there was laughter from our East Coast colleagues [international headquarters staff]." At Catholic Health Partners in Ohio, SEIU reached an agreement with the hospital system in which neither side would campaign at all. According to the National Labor Relations Board, "The only materials distributed to employees were jointly-created materials explaining the election process." The results of the election, reported on January 28, 2011, were that only four units out of forty-three (and only 10.2% of the workforce) voted to unionize.[6] If nothing else, this result suggests the ongoing importance of worker organizing and worker education to union success.

The international's focus on organizing was a double-edged sword. On the one hand, Stern's singular focus and take-no-prisoners approach helped to unsettle a languishing labor movement and organize tens of thousands of new members;[7] on the other hand, his approach was deliberately undemocratic, creating waves of organizational crisis in order to concentrate power and make decisions unilaterally.[8] SEIU's innovative organizing strategies have led to remarkable victories like the Justice for Janitors campaign in Los Angeles;[9] at the same time, these strategies seem constrained by an "ideology of organizing"[10] that considers union membership an end in itself—rather than a means to a broader vision of social justice (see conclusion).

Resistance from Within

Przeworski assumed that socialist parties played an important role in constructing workers' identities, leaving little possibility of resistance—from workers or from a dissenting faction of the party itself. Within SEIU, however, local leaders were upset by the international's willingness to compromise workers' ability to strike and workers' capacity to advocate for changes on the shop floor. According to a local organizer, the union would become nothing more than a "machine for growth." He asked, "Does it ultimately build power for working people? No, I don't think it does." Another local organizer agreed, saying, "I'm for growth as much as anybody. That's what I've spent most of my life trying to do. [But] it's gotta be something that's principled, and that makes sense." Not only did political compromises and alliances with management undermine workers' rights, but they removed the motivation workers had for being in a union at all.

Contrasting the international's conception of unionism with the local, a third organizer suggested that the international was just like the Sisters of St. Joseph of Orange:

> There are people in the Church who have a top-down approach to what the Catholic Church is. That it's a group of bishops. . . . And that's who the Church is, and they dictate to the rest of us what the Church is. And then there's a group of people who think the Church—it comes from the Greek word *ecclesia*, which just means place or building or people . . . a sense of community—is from the ground up. And that's always been resisted, just like [the resistance facing] what Sal [Rosselli]'s trying to build.

Sal Rosselli spoke in similar terms in an interview:

> There is a fundamental difference in ideology. The way we describe it is it's a bottom-up perspective versus a top-down perspective. We believe in empowering workers and that there is no limit to empowering them. This differs from SEIU's leadership who are increasingly concentrating power, their authority and resources among a few in Washington D.C.[11]

The local emphasized the importance of worker leadership and worker voice. Although local organizers' comments should be taken with a grain or two of salt, given that they were fighting the international and so had reason to emphasize the distinctions between them, they do raise important questions about what might be lost in a highly centralized labor organization. According to an organizer with the local, social change was impossible "if workers are basically [made] unaware of the potential they have for change by the very institutions that are supposed to be fostering and awakening them." Local leaders emphasized that the union's power was derived less from its agility in the political arena and more from workers' capacity to advocate for themselves. Another organizer suggested that the union was important not only to give people a higher standard of living but to give people "control over your life." Since "you spend a third of your life at work, that's going to affect you." Explaining the importance of workplace control, a third organizer quoted from a book he had read in which a worker had said, "The work rules, that's for me, as a worker. The wages and benefits, that's to take care of the family."

The ideological differences between the international and the local were mirrored elsewhere in organized labor, particularly in those segments committed to revitalization. And throughout the labor movement there seemed to be little room for disagreement. Dissent was understood as disloyalty, and politics took the place of process.[12] The creative strategies that unions used against employers were turned against one another, to ill effect. For example, the merger between the Union of Needletrades, Industrial and Textile Employees (UNITE) and the Hotel Employees and Restaurant Employees Union (HERE) unraveled after less than five years as differences in organizational culture and approach to organizing became apparent.[13] In an especially pernicious turn, in January of 2009—around the same time as the trusteeship of UHW—Stern and SEIU sided against HERE, its longtime ally, supporting the secession of former UNITE members (and UNITE's former president Bruce Raynor) into a newly formed SEIU subsidiary.[14]

Tensions built more gradually between UHW and the international. In 2003, the international brokered a deal with a coalition of nursing homes called the California Nursing Home Alliance, most of which were within the jurisdiction of the local union. Under the agreement, the union would help lobby the California Legislature to increase reimbursement rates for nursing home care. In exchange, the nursing home alliance would select forty-two homes to be organized by the union under "template agreements."[15] These agreements limited the extent to which workers would be able to bargain collectively, and put limitations on workplace grievances or public advocacy. Moreover, workers at nursing homes in the alliance were not permitted to organize outside of those homes that the nursing home companies permitted. A leader in the local union remembered advising that "there were some serious problems" with the deal, but he was willing to give it a chance to work. Brandon recalled the feeling around the local: "We're not totally cool with this but we also haven't been able to organize nursing homes in a way we know we need to, so let's give this a try."

Many in the local soon came to believe, however, that the nursing home industry could not be trusted. According to one local organizer, "We tried it, it didn't work, and it didn't work largely because nursing home owners are not honest." Yet the "international was still willing to work with them," leaving the local feeling that the international had bargained away the union's capacity to advocate for its members and for the patients the members served. In conversations with nursing home leaders, it became clear to local staff that the industry wanted to "eliminate shop-floor fights, shop-floor militancy." Stern's protégé, Tyrone Freeman, who had been handpicked to be president of what was then SEIU Local 434B, had been willing to give managerial control to the industry in exchange for better wages. According to a UHW leader, Freeman said to the industry, "You can manage this place, I don't care what shifts people work. . . . You pay them what we need, and you give us [the union] new [nursing] homes, and we'll figure it out." A memo the local sent to the international on September 22, 2005, expressed concern with the relationship between the union and the nursing home alliance. The local felt that it had expended large amounts of political capital for the rights to organize only forty homes: "It is important to note that 8,000 nursing home workers will benefit from the power of 600,000 SEIU members in California. This was the result of our SEIU State Council making rate reform the #1 priority legislatively." Moreover, the local expressed concern that the industry was wedded to maintaining template agreements that gave only minimal wage increases and restricted workers' rights on the floor: "The template is what sold them on the Alliance deal—labor peace at a low price."

Perhaps most controversially, in 2004 the international union reapproached the nursing home alliance to begin collaborative work on tort reform in the industry, in exchange for the industry's permission to organize a hundred more homes. In a memo sent from the local to the international, the local argued that the tort reform deal was "bad politics, bad policy, and a bad internal process." Many in the local agreed that tort reform was needed,[16] yet believed the deal forged between the international and the nursing home industry failed to protect nursing home patients—limiting patients' rights to sue without increasing other protections. Moreover, local leaders thought the deal would alienate the union from progressive allies around the state and country. A *San Francisco Weekly* exposé by Matt Smith in June 2004 derailed the efforts,[17] but not before embarrassing both the local and the international unions. In the article, UHW president Sal Rosselli defended the alliance agreement: "Traditionally, there has been an adversarial relationship between SEIU and general health care providers. We've been changing those relationships to accomplish common goals."

Divisions between the local and the international became public, however, when Smith published a second article in April 2007: "Officials with Sal Rosselli's UHW-West have apparently taken a strong stand saying corporate-friendly alliances aren't the panacea Stern makes them out to be."[18] The piece cited an internal memo by the local critical of the alliance deal. International staffers were convinced that Rosselli or other top local leaders were behind the story, although local leaders deny those claims to this day. The alliance was soon history. And it was that moment— according to many local leaders—when the international union decided, "We have to take them out."

From this point on the conflict took on the feel of a civil war, replete with intrigues, accusations, and acts of aggression. In early 2008, the international brokered a deal with nine Catholic hospitals in Ohio.[19] The hospitals, all part of the Catholic Healthcare Partners system, had agreed not to campaign against SEIU if the union would agree not to campaign for the union or build worker leadership leading up to the vote. Several outside unions were concerned that the arrangement was a "sweetheart deal," an arrangement that would lead to a weak bargaining position for the newly established union. In March, just before the scheduled elections, organizers from the California Nurses Association arrived to campaign against the deal, and the agreement fell apart. Yet the rumor among international leaders was that Sal Rosselli and the United Healthcare Workers West local was behind the "raid."

In response to Rosselli's perceived disloyalty, the international increasingly encroached on the local's decision-making authority. In December

2007 the international union orchestrated the removal of Rosselli as the head of SEIU's California State Council (Rosselli resigned before he could be removed). And by the spring of 2008 it became clear that Stern intended to remove long-term care workers from UHW, transferring approximately sixty-five thousand members out of the local and into a new long-term care "mega-local." Stern argued that the transfer was "consistent with [the union's] overall policy: to form larger locals that have greater bargaining and political power." He argued that the move "resembled a 2005 merger that benefited Mr. Rosselli, when a health care local in Southern California merged with his old local, with Mr. Rosselli heading the combined local."[20] Rosselli and many in the local, however, saw it as an effort at retaliation. In August, news broke that Tyrone Freeman, president of California's United Long-Term Care Workers Local and the intended recipient of UHW's long-term care members, had arranged for his wife and mother-in-law to receive hundreds of thousands of dollars in union contracts and donations.[21] Freeman was forced to resign, leaving California's largest union local without a leader. The international accused Rosselli of leaking the story to the *Los Angeles Times.*[22] At SEIU's 2008 National Convention, in Puerto Rico, the union ratified a platform that established nationwide councils to plan strategy for organizing campaigns, and increased the international's capacity to discipline dissident locals and redraw union boundaries. For Rosselli and others in the opposition, these measures seemed "designed to stifle dissent."[23]

In the fall of 2008, SEIU scheduled hearings to explore a trusteeship of UHW, accusing the local of financial malpractice and undermining union democracy. According to former UHW leaders, the local was worried about an impending trusteeship and had used members' dues to set up a "defense fund" that had been hidden from the international union. The hearing officer (appointed by the international office), former secretary of labor Ray Marshall, found that "those actions were not reason to impose a trusteeship but merely symptoms of the underlying conflict."[24] Nevertheless, Marshall recommended that the local be placed in trusteeship if it did not heed the international's order to transfer the sixty-five thousand nursing home and home care workers. "No democratic labor organization can permit local unions to nullify international decisions reached through the democratic processes specified in their constitution and bylaws," Marshall wrote in his decision.[25] On January 27, 2009, SEIU formally placed the local in trusteeship. On January 28, local staff and worker leaders announced the formation of the National Union of Healthcare Workers (NUHW), with the intention of decertifying the local (now in trusteeship) and moving workers into "a new, democratic union, with members in control."[26]

The Story in Santa Rosa

The union's struggle with St. Joseph Health System did not fit neatly into the dichotomy that came to characterize the struggle between the local and the international. A synthesis between the two conceptions of unionism seemed to make the campaign possible. One union leader on the campaign discussed how she saw the two sides in the conflict as being consistent with and complementary to one another:

> [Stern] is an elected representative who's doing his best to represent the interests of workers in his union and those he would like to be in his union. So he's a visionary, dedicated labor leader. And he might even say it's his fiduciary responsibility to grow this union. . . . You have to make compromises and that's the art form, and that's all true. And Sal Rosselli can say I have fiduciary responsibility to my membership in California on whose back you want to make these compromises. And I want workers at the table in every bargaining [session]. And struggle is good because it fortifies the base. I don't want to cut a deal. I want the workers to claim it, own it. Ownership. Are they mutually exclusive? I would argue that they don't have to be. They can be complementary.

In the two years leading up to the trusteeship, however, the Catholic strategy was undermined because of divisions between the local and the international. In the fall of 2007, as the local prepared for its largest march to date in Orange County, Ross and Goldstein received a call from the international's representative at the national Catholic roundtable asking them to call the march off. According to the representative, it was "causing some problems at the national table." Ross and Goldstein answered that they would be open to putting a moratorium on public action if the system was serious about sitting down—which the system made clear it was not. A few months later, facilitators at the national table approached the local again in an effort to stop the local's St. Joseph Health System campaign, since SJHS was threatening to withdraw from the national roundtable. Ross saw an opportunity to generate counterpressure on Deborah Proctor and SJHS executives, letting "her and the Sisters know that they were in violation of the core principles" of the national agreement. International leaders again demurred, telling Ross that the strategy he had proposed was "impossible."

Ross would later learn from an international leader in the union's healthcare division that the international union made a decision *not* to support the St. Joseph Health System campaign as early as August 2008, worrying that a victory for the local would make trusteeship more difficult. Moreover, throughout the fall of 2008—the very moment SJHS first expressed willingness to negotiate—CHA president Sister Carol Keehan had been advising the Sisters of St. Joseph of Orange not to engage with the local, citing the conflict between the local and the international. According to Ross, such advice would almost certainly have come from the international union itself.

Workers on Their Own

A couple of weeks after trusteeship, Ross, Purcell, and I drove to St. Helena for a meeting with Monsignor Brenkle to discuss the disintegration of the St. Joseph Health System campaign. On our way to the rectory, we passed a newspaper stand, and the front page stopped us in our tracks: due to a $17.7 million dollar shortfall in its Sonoma County operations, SJHS was planning to lay off 152 workers from Santa Rosa Memorial Hospital within the next two months.[27] The next day, Ross approached the international about fighting the layoffs with a remaining SEIU organizer who had worked on the SJHS campaign. Such a crisis at Memorial might help rekindle organizing efforts there. Yet the organizer was told that SJHS workers were "no longer a priority." Mari, a member of the organizing committee, recalled her anger when the union "closed our offices, never responded to our phone calls, never called us, never answered us.... They disappeared off the face of earth." What was hardest for her was losing credibility among her co-workers: "It's really hard to walk down those hallways, and those employees for years you've been telling them you can help them to get a voice. . . . You feel that they are looking at you and they're thinking, 'You're full [of it].'" Mari was also one of the workers who received a layoff notice: "So I got hit not only emotionally from SEIU, my co-workers lost credibility in me, they were looking at me like 'you fool,' and then I lost my job. When I lost my job, there was no one from SEIU to advise me. . . . I've been fighting for you for the last six years, telling them SEIU was good. Where is SEIU for me?"

Within days of the trusteeship Brandon, the lead organizer on the campaign since 2005, held a meeting with workers to discuss the options: continue to organize with SEIU, organize with the newly formed NUHW, or throw in the towel. Many were angry with SEIU, but unsure about the new union. After all, the new union did not have any money, any members, or any real staff. But after several days and some debate, the committee voted unanimously to go with NUHW. After having collected 60 percent of the signatures needed to file for a union representation election with SEIU-UHW before trusteeship, the committee would have to start over. Dan recalled thinking, "Okay, we'll push the rock up the hill again." Brandon described the organizing committee's reaction: "'Oh Christ, we have to go back and do this again, it's going to be hard, I don't know if we can do it,' but it was the only option that people felt good about, especially after SEIU didn't return their phone calls."

This time around, workers had to make do without the formidable resources that SEIU-UHW once offered. The paid staff in Santa Rosa went from a high of six (give or take) in 2007 to zero. Brandon was now officially unemployed, but agreed to continue on as a volunteer. Workers gave him gas money and an occasional stipend out of their own pockets. Without an office, the committee met in the clubhouse at one of the worker's condominium developments. Without any copy machines, workers would print flyers illicitly at work or foot the bills themselves.

But the new union's lack of resources actually seemed to inspire a kind of resourcefulness, helping workers take ownership of the campaign more fully. Brandon remembered, "It's the little things that probably they would have done the whole time anyway, but because we have money, because we have an infrastructure of resources we don't expect people to do that, so when people are willing to do that kind of stuff for themselves it's always pretty remarkable." Brandon said that "it really felt like you were part of one of the great labor struggles of our day . . . you think about the farmworkers, and everybody working for free." Mari drew a similar comparison when she spoke of the new union's lack of resources, explaining, "Cesar Chavez didn't have the resources when he began." Organizing committee members recalled feeling that they owned the campaign in a different way. Frank remembered explaining to people that the decision to go with NUHW meant that "we're the union" even more fully. Brandon explained that in a long campaign "you keep going because that's what you've been doing. It almost becomes a habit. . . . And to have that all of a sudden feel exciting and new after five years is pretty amazing." Without union resources to support them, workers were forced to draw on new sources of intrinsic motivation and to take on new leadership roles.

Members of the organizing committee went to speak with their co-workers once again, and over the course of the next two months managed to re-create their petition support, this time with NUHW. On April 13, 2009, more than four years after the previous election was scheduled, they filed with the National Labor Relations Board—demonstrating close to 60 percent support of all the eligible workers. SEIU-UHW quickly intervened, charging NUHW with unfair labor practices and postponing the election.[28] Through such legal maneuvers, SEIU was able to put off the election until December 19, 2009. Somewhat hypocritically, given the international's interest in "fair election" agreements, SEIU was also able to stave off any such agreement in Santa Rosa. In September 2009, SEIU-UHW stated that it would not enter into any sort of election agreement with NUHW and SJHS. In late November, Robert Reich and Monsignor John Brenkle offered to bring the parties together to negotiate election ground rules. This time SJHS and NUHW accepted the offer, but SEIU refused.

For members of the organizing committee, the last-minute intervention by SEIU was infuriating—and motivating. Cynthia recalled that it felt as if the hospital and SEIU were both "taking away [workers'] right" to a fair election. Yet while workers had ambivalent feelings about the hospital as a whole, SEIU was more clearly "an enemy" and so helped to "galvanize" the organizing committee: "It became more obvious that [SEIU] didn't really have workers' interest at heart. And that seemed really important to me to stand up to, above and beyond our own local fight." More than they ever had before, workers at Memorial suddenly felt the national implications of their efforts.

For their part, SEIU organizers in Santa Rosa argued that they had the resources to win results for workers—and that NUHW would likely be bankrupt before winning a contract. According to Mari, SEIU "told us that they had the money, their money and their power will make us be successful. But there was nothing about your voice is going to make you successful. It was 'our money,' SEIU's money is going to make you successful." SEIU demonstrated its resources by sending eight organizers to Santa Rosa in the months preceding the election. In the weeks prior to the election, SEIU brought workers from other SEIU organized hospitals into Memorial's cafeteria wearing bright yellow T-shirts with "Truth Squad" printed across the front. And in a move strangely reminiscent of the Orange County blitz that I had taken part in two years before, SEIU organized a blitz at Santa Rosa Memorial Hospital in which three-hundred union members and organizers reached out to workers a few weeks before the scheduled election. The gathered crowd also held an "informational picket" outside the hospital.

Despite SEIU's resources, it was unable to get any traction with Memorial workers. For several weeks SEIU organizers held informational meetings at their office in Santa Rosa. At the first meeting no workers showed up aside from NUHW hecklers. At the second meeting, one Memorial worker came to find out more about SEIU, yet four NUHW committee members were there to greet him. As SEIU organizers tried to separate the one worker from the committee members, Andrew remembered, the committee members resisted, and began to "educate him on how horrible SEIU was." By the end of the meeting, NUHW had gained another organizing committee member.

But winning the election, it seemed, was never SEIU's intention in Santa Rosa. Rather, SEIU hoped to prevent NUHW from gaining any momentum. International trustee Dave Regan explained SEIU's strategy more crassly in a meeting of organizers in Fresno when he told them SEIU needed "to drive a stake through the heart of the thing that is NUHW," to "put them in the ground and bury them."[29] As Dan explained of his co-workers, "A lot of people went, 'Unions, a pox on both their houses.' And that was [SEIU's] whole intent when they came here. I think they realized from the get-go they didn't have a shot." Unsurprisingly, those against *any* union at Memorial had a field day with the internecine fight. Around the time that NUHW filed for an election, hospital management posted a memo citing a statement by SEIU international leader Eliseo Medina: "According to top SEIU officers, the leaders of SEIU/UHW-West were found to have violated their duties to their membership, engaged in serious financial wrongdoing, attempted to subvert the democratic processes of the union, and failed to safeguard collective bargaining relationships." In mid November, a flyer circulating among antiunion staff at the hospital depicted SEIU and NUHW as two burning houses, alongside a plea for "help and advice from anyone to keep these troublemakers away."

The election was scheduled for December 17–18. By the time of the vote count, the organizing committee was almost delirious with exhaustion. According to Brandon, no one had slept more than four hours per night in the previous seventy-two hours. By the time the polls closed at 4:30 p.m., Andrew had been up for twenty-four hours. The count took place in the hospital's Life Learning Center, across the street from the main building. But as workers approached, Brandon recalled, "management turned it into a police state," posting several security guards in and around the building. Rebecca was turned away because she had forgotten her hospital identification in her car. Children and spouses initially were refused entry as well. And by the time workers made it past security and into the room where the count was to take place, they found that the front rows had been occupied by managers and antiunion workers. Brandon looked back on the night with some anger: "They treat their own employees like criminals, not like people who we trust taking care of our children and our loved ones and our parents. It's disgusting. You're good enough to help someone deliver a baby, but you're not good enough to watch your own vote count."

Then the count began. An NLRB administrator read the ballots aloud one by one. It quickly became clear to everyone in the room that the contest was between NUHW and "no union." With only about thirty ballots remaining, "no union" had taken a significant lead over NUHW, and it seemed to many in the room that the remaining ballots would be "no union" as well. Andrew remembered seeing managers "having a good old time and chit-chatting back and forth, smiling." But the tide turned. The last ballots were all NUHW, bringing its grand total to 283 compared with 263 for "no union." SEIU had received thirteen votes in total. After more than five years of struggle, workers at Memorial had voted for their union.

Winning the Union before Winning the Union

How did workers with NUHW win in 2009 when the same workers could not win with SEIU-UHW in 2005? In 2005, workers had access to many more resources and more staff support; in 2005, there was no civil war within the labor movement. And although St. Joseph Health System theoretically had agreed to negotiate "fair election" ground rules in August 2008, no such agreement had been reached in either election campaign. Despite seemingly *less* favorable conditions in 2009, NUHW was able to win.

Several factors seemed to contribute to the victory. First, the very length of the struggle had helped to institutionalize the union in the minds of workers. According to Brandon, "Because the union had been there for five years, it was something people had gotten used to . . . and some managers at least had gotten used to." The union was no longer a group of outsiders but was *part* of the community of the hospital. Brandon himself, who had been working on the campaign since 2004, had become a familiar face. And the fact that many workers were willing to spend five years advocating for unionization helped to dispel the idea that the union was an outside third party.

Second, the union's cultural strategy had resulted in concrete concessions from management that helped to mitigate management's antiunion campaign. According to Brandon, "The boss didn't campaign in the same way that they did the first time." In 2005, the hospital had held mandatory meetings every week leading up to the election, and had built a "case against the union." In 2009, Brandon suggested, "because of the work that we did in the intervening period," management "never got strategic about it." Finally, workers felt that the community was behind them and their efforts. Religious leaders, political representatives, and other community figures had all consistently expressed their support for workers' right to organize. A vote for the union was no longer understood as a vote against the hospital, as it had been (at least for some) in the earlier campaign.

But workers' victory at the ballot box did not lead seamlessly to a first contract, or even to union recognition. Soon after the election, St. Joseph Health System appealed the results to the National Labor Relations Board, charging that the NUHW had campaigned unfairly, had "engaged in surveillance of employees," and that the NLRB itself had "displayed the employees' choices in different fonts and font styles thereby confusing voters and/or creating the impression that the NLRB disfavored the employer."[30] On May 28, 2010, the regional office of the NLRB overruled the objections "in their entirety," and certified NUHW "as the exclusive collective bargaining agent" at the hospital. Yet SJHS appealed the decision to the NLRB, further postponing recognition of the union. Scholars and NLRB administrators have documented the problem of delay at the NLRB, and its use by antiunion employers.[31]

SJHS's appeals were almost certainly out of line with principles agreed upon by the United States Conference of Catholic Bishops, however, who—in their working paper—had explicitly stated the need to avoid "using the law as a weapon or means of delay." All the more remarkably, on June 23, 2009, the Conference formalized its recommendations in a document entitled *Respecting the Just Rights of Workers: Guidance and Options for Catholic Health Care and Unions.* Yet NUHW had no way to appeal to the national table, a table at which SEIU remained a powerful force. It was only after the NLRB overturned this second appeal that St. Joseph Health System finally recognized the union on December 29, 2010—over a year after workers voted for the union, and over six years since workers started organizing. As of this writing in November of 2011, contract negotiations are still in process.

The workers' story at Santa Rosa Memorial Hospital is thus one of mixed success. Against all odds workers were able to win an election against an antiunion hospital system and against the most powerful labor union in the United States. But the same grassroots spirit that allowed them to win the election had left them relatively isolated as they approached the bargaining table. For some of the workers I interviewed, the lesson of their victory seemed to be that "smaller is better." For George, "big unions are almost like another big corporation." He hoped "that NUHW doesn't get so big that they lose their perspective." Mari echoed this sentiment, explaining that SEIU "lost track, they lost their own teaching . . . just like Memorial lost their teachings, the nuns lost their teachings. [SEIU] became a corporation too big for their own good." Both George and Mari seemed to suggest that NUHW's small scale is part of what allowed it to give workers voice.

But in a world of large national and international employers, a world of powerful and well-funded political parties and interest groups, there has to be a way for workers to win voice *and* collective power—to combine respect for the dignity of individual workers with collective power for workers as a group, if not a class.

CONCLUSION

What Should Unions Do?

As this book has shown, the struggle for unionization in the hospital industry—an industry in which workers tend to have a vocational relationship to their work, and that understands itself in terms irreducible to the market—raises fundamental questions about the labor movement in the twenty-first century.

To paraphrase the well-known study by Richard Freeman and James Medoff, *what should unions do?*[1] There is a vast scholarly literature exploring the material effects of unionization on its members. Unionization has long been observed to enhance members' economic well-being, increasing workers' wages and benefits substantially.[2] Recent research has suggested that workers in unions receive an average "wage premium" of 17.8 percent,[3] and are 28.2 percent more likely to receive health benefits than their nonunion counterparts.[4]

Beyond increases in wages and benefits, union membership assures a degree of job security, both in the sense that it increases a worker's propensity to use "voice" as opposed to "exit" as a strategy for resolving difficulties on the job[5] and it makes it more difficult for an employer to fire an employee at will. Indeed, despite the ethic of individual rights that pervades U.S. law and culture, U.S. citizens have almost no rights at work without collective representation. Without negotiated due-process protections, for example, workers can be fired for any reason, other than on the basis of age, sex, religion, or nationality, with no right to due process.[6] Unions thus help workers win rights in the workplace, help them negotiate disputes at work, and help ensure that workers who *do* speak up can do so without fear of reprisal.[7] Union membership has been shown to increase the annual number of hours that an employee works, and reduce firings and layoffs.[8]

These advantages to unionization are the foundations of a dignified work life. For good reason, then, whether struggling on the shop floor or in the political arena, union leaders and workers emphasize these benefits. Yet I have argued that in order to expand their influence and material effects, unions must go beyond these material foundations and be attuned to the cultural dimensions of labor struggle.

The essence of the argument I have made throughout the book is captured in figure 1. Unions must pay attention to both power and culture, and must understand the different ways that power and culture operate on the shop floor and in the broader economy. These two dimensions provide a framework for understanding the campaign to organize Santa Rosa Memorial Hospital. Chapter 1 demonstrated how the cultural values on which SRMH was founded continue to resonate with workers in the hospital, not only because workers' hearts are "managed" but also because of the interpersonal and vocational nature of hospital work. Chapter 2 described workers' first organizing efforts in the hospital, and the relationship between workers' desire for power and their emotional investments in their work—elements that I argue *can* be made consistent but are not necessarily so. The hospital administration was able to win the first round of the campaign not only by using standard antiunion strategies but also by appealing to those values of caring and compassion to which the union did not clearly speak.

At the end of chapter 2, I presented the story of the union's political struggle as it moved from the workplace to the political arena. This political strategy was an unsuccessful example of more standard "comprehensive campaigns" or "corporate campaigns," which use economic and political leverage to neutralize antiunion employers. Although these sorts

	Culture	Power
Corporate field	Ideology of capital	Economic and political power
Workplace	Workers' emotional investment in work	Workers' control

Figure 1. A framework for the book

of economic and political leverage are often important components of labor struggles, the SJHS campaign demonstrated their limits as well. Since St. Joseph Health System was an organization motivated by more than just the bottom line, the prospect of economic loss was not enough to change the system's behavior.

Chapters 3 and 4 discussed how the union shifted from a focus on workplace voice and political power to a deeper appreciation of the cultural dimensions of labor struggle. By articulating a compelling vision of Catholic social teaching around which religious leaders could organize, and by combining this argument with powerful worker stories of the "mobilized" heart, the union was able to win an unlikely victory on theological terrain.

Yet at almost the very moment the union won its campaign for a "fair election" agreement, internal conflicts tore apart the union itself. This was the focus of chapter 5. Although the local seemed to prioritize workplace voice and grassroots control, the international saw itself as a political actor working to advance workers' interests on the national stage.

The framework elaborated above is not only explanatory but also prescriptive. Unions in the twenty-first century must attend to all four dimensions of labor struggle, and must navigate the tensions that inevitably emerge between them. This is true not only within organizing campaigns but in labor unions' everyday practices as well. First, unions must wrestle with the meaning of work as it is experienced by workers. Workers' emotional investments should not be treated as false consciousness or the result of managerial manipulation, but rather should be understood as emerging out of the labor process itself. As Michael Burawoy writes, "it is lived experience that produces ideology, not the other way around. Ideology is rooted in and expresses the activities out of which it emerges."[9] Workers in the hospital (and elsewhere) who feel emotionally invested in the care they provide are not being fooled: these emotions emerge organically out of their interactions with patients and with one another.

Labor unions must appreciate the interpretive work of organizing, must help workers to see that the care in which they are invested is consistent with the struggle for more power within the hospital. Organizers must help workers move from the martyred heart to the mobilized heart. In his rich account of the relationship between labor unions and new social movements, Dan Clawson argues that unions must "fuse with [new social movements] such that it is no longer clear what is a 'labor' issue and what is a 'women's' issue or an 'immigrant' issue."[10] My analysis extends this perspective by arguing that unions must apply new social movements' appreciation of culture and identity to the shop floor itself.

Conversely, labor organizations must do more to substantiate the claim that worker power *is* actually consistent with care. Although healthcare unions have long found it rhetorically useful to suggest that unionization improves patient care, there is little evidence to date to support or refute this claim.[11] Indeed, the claim is made more difficult to substantiate by the fact that the National Labor Relations Act narrows the scope of mandatory bargaining to wages, hours, benefits, and working conditions, making negotiations over patient care difficult or impossible in most contexts.[12]

The concept of worker "voice" nicely bridges union's efforts to enhance worker control with the recognition of workers' investment in their work. As those at or near the bottom of the hospital's hierarchy, workers need voice in order to advocate for themselves and for patients, with whom they are often in close contact. Yet as contemporary unions use the word, "voice" risks becoming an empty cliché, a euphemism for worker power and control. Unions might spend more time thinking about and researching the ways that voice enhances and encumbers care, and train workers in how to use their voice in order to enhance their commitment to patients.

Granted, there are times when workers' emotional investments will inevitably feel in conflict with the desire for workplace power. Even in the hospital, the strike will likely never disappear as an important strategy in labor's arsenal, but the union can work to interpret strikes more clearly for workers and for the communities they affect. Likewise, however, there are times when unions must support workers' emotional investments at the expense of workplace power. The contract must be flexible enough to respect the covenant workers will continue to feel with their patients. Moreover, the tension between the two should be a source of ongoing discussion and debate as unions decide on strategy. Describing one success story, Thomas A. Kochan and his colleagues demonstrate how the labor-management partnership at Kaiser Permanente helps to facilitate an interest-based bargaining approach that allows both labor and management to think outside the "black box" of the NLRA.[13]

Just as workers' emotional investments must be taken seriously, so should the ideological character of the corporation. In the St. Joseph Health System campaign, the religious commitments of the hospital system leadership had some degree of autonomy from the organization's economic interests—autonomy that provided the union with a new arena of struggle. Although ideology in the form of Catholic theology may be more readily apparent in a Catholic hospital than in other sorts of corporations, it is important for unions to recognize the ways in which all corporations (and unions themselves!) exist within cultural worlds that can provide unlikely and previously unrecognized openings. Some of the most successful organizing campaigns in recent years have challenged conventional meanings of both "worker" and "employer."[14]

Likewise, the labor movement must self-consciously combine a concern for political and economic power with a cultural argument about what kind of society is possible. Bill Fletcher and Fernando Gapasin observe that an "ideology of organizing," or a focus on expansion for its own sake, has emerged within the labor movement at least in part as a result of the absence of a contemporary vision of a "Left project."[15] The union's attention to the cultural dimension of capital must also involve the articulation of an *alternative* vision of what work should mean, and how it should be organized, in the twenty-first century. Given this project, there are times when the union must sacrifice some of its power for the consistency of its cultural argument. For example, blocking the construction of acute-care hospitals does not sit well with the idea that unions stand for better health-care. On the other hand, there are times when political expediency and power must take priority over cultural consistency. But these times must be chosen deliberately and self-consciously.

Finally, unions must manage the inevitable tensions between bottom-up and top-down strategies. Without worker participation and leadership, the labor movement risks becoming little more than an interest group working on behalf of workers. Former SEIU president Andy Stern wrote almost as much when he described his job as being to "watch out for the threats that confront our members—and all American workers."[16] Not only does the labor movement begin to sound like the AARP in Stern's account, but he also presumes a personal capacity to accurately represent the interests of the working class on his own. The iron law of oligarchy, broken briefly,[17] again rears its ugly head.[18] On the other hand, without some degree of centralization and large-scale strategy, victories like the one at Santa Rosa Memorial Hospital risk becoming footnotes in the broader story of union decline. While it took six years to win union recognition for the workers at Santa Rosa Memorial Hospital, the Bureau of Labor Statistics estimates that the hospital industry will expand by over half a million workers (of all classifications) between 2008 and 2018.[19] As Ruth Milkman observes, "In the current environment, with a power imbalance between management and labor more extreme than it has been anytime since the birth of the New Deal, unions can be effective only by combining top-down and bottom-up traditions."[20]

The four faces to labor struggle present tensions for the labor movement in the twenty-first century, tensions that must be managed rather than resolved. And while there are no easy organizational solutions, one place in which these tensions might be discussed, debated, and made productive rather than destructive is in the context of membership education. Bill Fletcher and Fernando Gapasin rightly suggest that many unions "see membership education . . . as a means of communicating the message of the leadership to the membership."[21] Instead, they argue that this sort of education should "provide a framework that members can use to analyze their experiences and guide actions in their own interests."[22] I would add that this sort of education should be reciprocal, in that worker leaders have important insights into their own workplaces and might help bridge the values and motivations of their co-workers and the broader social justice vision of the union. In his study of the success of the United Farm Workers, Marshall Ganz argues that an organization's "strategic capacity" is enhanced when people from different backgrounds strategize together.[23] Particularly when confronting new problems, diverse groups can access different resources, bring different skills to bear, and generate more creative solutions. Creating spaces within the union for these sorts of discussions and debates would help avoid the perils of either top-down autocracy or bottom-up utopianism. They also would help to bridge the union's focus on power with a sensitivity to the experiences and meanings that workers themselves bring to the struggle.

What should unions mean for the workers who belong to them? What vision of society should unions be striving toward? The story at Santa Rosa Memorial Hospital is simultaneously a compelling example of union success and a useful prism through which to ask these broader questions about the labor movement.

NOTES

Preface

1. Farm workers had been excluded from the Wagner Act.
2. Eileen Purcell, "Psalm of a Low Wage Worker," in *Prayers for the New Social Awakening: Inspired by the New Social Creed*, ed. Christian Isso and Elizabeth Hinson-Hasty (Louisville, Ky.: Westminster John Knox Press, 2008), 115.

Introduction

1. Until 2008, the highest level of decision-making authority in the system had resided with a "Sponsorship Board" consisting entirely of Sisters. During this time the Sisters also made up a majority on the system's board of directors. In 2004, however, the Sisters applied to the Vatican to establish a "public juridic person," a lay body with which the Sisters could share governance responsibilities (see Judy Cassidy, "St. Joseph Health System Looks Forward to New Life as a Public Juridic Person," *Health Progress* [November–December 2004], 6–10). This body attained formal authority on May 10, 2008 ("St. Joseph System Marks Transition to New Sponsorship Structure," *Catholic Health World* 24:14 [August 1, 2008]). As of 2011, this new board consisted of three Sisters and two lay leaders.
2. Bureau of Labor Statistics, "Career Guide to Industries, 2010–2011 Edition: Healthcare," http://www.bls.gov/oco/cg/cgs035.htm#related.
3. Catholic Health Association of the United States, "Catholic Health Care in the United States" (Washington, D.C.: 2011).

4. Rosemary Stevens, *American Medicine and the Public Interest: A History of Specialization* (New Haven: Yale University Press, 1971).

5. W. Richard Scott et al., *Institutional Change and Healthcare Organizations: From Professional Dominance to Managed Care* (Chicago: University of Chicago Press, 2000).

6. In 2010, 14.3 percent of workers in hospitals were members of unions, the most of any segment of the health care and social assistance industries and slightly more than the 12.3 percent' of workers who were members of unions across the U.S. workforce: see Barry Hirsch and David Macpherson, *Union Membership and Earnings Databook: Compilations from the Current Population Survey* (Arlington, Va.: Bureau of National Affairs, 2010).

7. When workers in New York City hospitals began organizing in the late 1950s, Fred K. Fish, president of Greater New York Hospital Association, argued for the impropriety of unions in hospitals: "Voluntary hospitals have accepted responsibility of the sick and are committed to this obligation. They cannot delegate any part of this responsibility to a union or any other medically unrelated organization. . . . There should be no intervention when the issue may be life or death": Leon Fink and Brian Greenberg, *Upheaval in the Quiet Zone: A History of Hospital Workers' Union, Local 1199* (Chicago: University of Illinois Press, 1989), 54. Similar arguments continue to appear today.

8. Paul Johnston, *Success While Others Fail: Social Movement Unionism and the Public Workplace* (Ithaca, N.Y.: ILR Press, 1994).

9. Suzanne Gordon, *Nursing against the Odds: How Health Care Cost Cutting, Media Stereotypes, and Medical Hubris Undermine Nurses and Patient Care* (Ithaca: Cornell University Press, 2005), 295.

10. Union leaders cited Martin Luther King Jr.'s 1963 "Letter from Birmingham Jail" as a powerful response to the argument that worker leaders and union organizers brought conflict to the hospital. In the letter, written to eight white Alabama clergymen who had opposed civil rights demonstrations, King argued: "You deplore the demonstrations taking place in Birmingham. But your statement, I am sorry to say, fails to express a similar concern for the conditions that brought about the demonstrations. I am sure that none of you would want to rest content with the superficial kind of social analysis that deals merely with effects and does not grapple with underlying causes. It is unfortunate that demonstrations are taking place in Birmingham, but it is even more unfortunate that the city's white power structure left the Negro community with no alternative" (James M. Washington, ed., *The Essential Writings and Speeches of Martin Luther King, Jr.* [New York: HarperCollins], 289–302).

11. Sioban Nelson, *Say Little, Do Much: Nursing, Nuns, and Hospitals in the Nineteenth Century* (Philadelphia: University of Pennsylvania Press, 2001), 6.

12. Eileen Purcell, "St. Joseph Health System Workers' Organizing Campaign," SEIU campaign history, 2009. In author's files.

13. A comparative case design has been used productively in several recent studies of labor movement success. See Jennifer Jihye Chun, *Organizing at the Margins: The Symbolic Politics of Labor in South Korea and the United States* (Ithaca: Cornell University Press, 2009); Marshall Ganz, *Why David Sometimes Wins: Leadership, Organization, and Strategy in the California Farm Worker Movement* (New York: Oxford University Press, 2009); Marshall Ganz, "Resources and Resourcefulness: Strategic Capacity in the Unionization of California Agriculture, 1959–1966," *American Journal of Sociology* 105:4 (2000): 1003–62; Steven Henry Lopez, *Reorganizing the Rust Belt: An Inside Study of the American Labor Movement* (Berkeley: University of California Press, 2004).

14. Arlie Hochschild, *The Managed Heart: Commercialization of Human Feeling* (Berkeley: University of California Press, 1983).

15. Ibid., 35.

16. Rachel Sherman, *Class Acts: Service and Inequality in Luxury Hotels* (Berkeley: University of California Press, 2007).

17. Steven Henry Lopez, "Emotional Labor and Organized Emotional Care: Conceptualizing Nursing Home Care Work," *Work and Occupations* 33:2 (2006): 133–60; Martin B. Tolich, "Alienating and Liberating Emotions at Work: Supermarket Clerks' Performance of Customer Service," *Journal of Contemporary Ethnography* 22:3 (1993): 361–81.

18. Hochschild, *Managed Heart*, 21.

19. Barbara Ehrenreich and John Ehrenreich, "Hospital Workers: Class Conflicts in the Making," *International Journal of Health Services* 5:1 (1975): 43–51.

20. Paula England, Michelle Budig, and Nancy Folbre, "Wages of Virtue: The Relative Pay of Care Work," *Social Problems* 49:4 (2002): 458.

21. Michael Burawoy, *Manufacturing Consent: Changes in the Labor Process under Monopoly Capitalism* (Chicago: University of Chicago Press, 1979).

22. Rick Fantasia, *Cultures of Solidarity: Consciousness, Action, and Contemporary American Unions* (Berkeley: University of California Press, 1988).

23. Ibid., 132.

24. Ibid., 138.

25. Kate Bronfenbrenner, "Employer Behavior in Certification Elections and First Contracts: Implications for Labor Law Reform," in *Restoring the Promise of American Labor Law*, ed. Sheldon Friedman et al. (Ithaca, N.Y.: ILR Press, 1994), 75–89; Dan Clawson, *The Next Upsurge: Labor and the New Social Movements* (Ithaca: Cornell University Press, 2003); Julius G. Getman, *Restoring the Power of Unions: It Takes a Movement* (New Haven: Yale University Press, 2010); Sanford M. Jacoby, ed., *Masters to Managers: Historical and Comparative Perspectives on American Employers* (New York: Columbia University Press, 1991).

26. Larry Cohen and Richard W. Hurd, "Fear, Conflict, and Union Organizing," in *Organizing to Win: New Research on Union Strategies*, ed. Kate Bronfenbrenner et al. (Ithaca: Cornell University Press, 1998), 181–96; Richard B. Freeman and Joel Rogers, *What Workers Want* (Ithaca: Cornell University Press, 1999).

27. Fantasia, *Cultures of Solidarity*, 17.

28. Ibid., 19.

29. Johnston, *Success While Others Fail*, 116.

30. Ibid., 140.

31. Gordon, *Nursing Against the Odds*, 296.

32. Ehrenreich and Ehrenreich, "Hospital Workers"; John P. Hoerr, *We Can't Eat Prestige: The Women Who Organized Harvard* (Philadelphia: Temple University Press, 2001); Clawson, *Next Upsurge*, 81.

33. Christopher Bryan-Brown and Kathleen Dracup, "Professionalism," *American Journal of Critical Care* 12 (2003): 395.

34. Ibid., 395.

35. Michael Ash and Jean Ann Seago, "The Effect of Registered Nurses' Unions on Heart-Attack Mortality," *Industrial and Labor Relations Review* 57:3 (2004): 422–42.

36. Suzanne Gordon, John Buchanan, and Tanya Bretherton. *Safety in Numbers: Nurse-to-Patient Ratios and the Future of Healthcare* (Ithaca: Cornell University Press, 2008).

37. Bryan-Brown and Dracup, "Professionalism," 395.

38. Getman, *Restoring the Power of Unions*, chap. 10.

39. Kate Bronfenbrenner and Tom Juravich, "It Takes More Than House Calls: Organizing to Win with a Comprehensive Union-Building Strategy," in *Organizing to Win*, 19–36; Clawson, *Next Upsurge;* Getman, *Restoring the Power of Unions;* Pierrette Hondagneu-Sotelo, *God's Heart Has No Borders: How Religious Activists Are Working for Immigrant Rights* (Berkeley: University of

California Press, 2008); Lopez, *Reorganizing the Rust Belt*; Ruth Milkman, *L.A. Story: Immigrant Workers and the Future of the U.S. Labor Movement* (New York: Russell Sage Foundation, 2006).

40. See http://www.starbucks.com/career-center/working-at-starbucks; http://walmartstores.com/Careers/; see Thomas A. Kochan, Harry C. Katz, and Robert B. Kersie, *The Transformation of American Industrial Relations* (New York: Basic Books, 1986).

41. Charles Hughes, *Making Unions Unnecessary* (New York: Executive Enterprises Publications, 1976); Sanford Jacoby, *Employing Bureaucracy: Managers, Unions, and the Transformation of Work in American Industry, 1900–1945* (New York: Columbia University Press, 1985); Jacoby, *Masters to Managers*; John Logan, "The Union Avoidance Industry in the United States," *British Journal of Industrial Relations* 44:4 (2006): 651–75; James Rundle, "Winning Hearts and Minds in the Era of Employee-Involvement Programs," in *Organizing to Win*, 213–31.

42. Jarol Manheim, *The Death of a Thousand Cuts: Corporate Campaigns and the Attack on the Corporation* (New York: Routledge, 2000).

43. Rosemary Stevens, *In Sickness and in Wealth: American Hospitals in the Twentieth Century* (New York: Basic Books, 1989), 164. Hospital workers became exempt from the National Labor Relations Act after the passage of the Taft-Hartley Act in 1947.

44. Ibid., 164.

45. Many union leaders expressed frustration that their use of theology would be questioned, feeling as though their own religious backgrounds had been stripped of them by the Sisters. They pointed out that Cesar Chavez and the United Farm Workers were not charged with using religious teaching instrumentally, and believed that a labor movement worth working for *had* to tie economic interests to a broader moral vision.

46. Chun, *Organizing at the Margins*; Ganz, *Why David Sometimes Wins*; Hondagnu-Soleto, *God's Heart Has No Borders*:; Lopez, *Reorganizing the Rust Belt*; Randy Shaw, *Beyond the Fields: Cesar Chavez, the UFW, and the Struggle for Justice in the 21st Century* (Berkeley: University of California Press, 2008).

47. Doug McAdam, John McCarthy, and Mayer Zald, eds., *Comparative Perspectives on Social Movements: Political Opportunities, Mobilizing Structures, and Cultural Framings* (New York: Cambridge University Press, 1996); Snow et al., "Frame Alignment Processes, Micromobilization, and Movement Participation," *American Sociological Review* 51:4 (1986): 464–81; David Snow and Robert Benford, "Clarifying the Relationship between Framing and Ideology," *Mobilization* 5:1 (2000): 55–60.

48. Snow and Benford, "Clarifying the Relationship between Framing and Ideology," 614.

49. Doug McAdam and W. Richard Scott, "Organizations and Movements," in Gerald F. Davis et al., eds. *Social Movements and Organizational Theory* (New York: Cambridge University Press, 2005).

50. Marc Steinberg, "Tilting the Frame: Framing from a Discursive Turn," *Sociological Theory* 27:6 (1998), 556.

51. Marc Steinberg, "The Talk and Back Talk of Collective Action: A Dialogic Analysis of Repertoires of Discourse among Nineteenth-Century Cotton Spinners," *American Journal of Sociology* 105 (1999); 751.

52. Antonio Gramsci, *Further Selections from the Prison Notebooks*, trans. and ed. Derek Boothman (Minnesota: University of Minnesota Press, 1995).

53. Ibid., 126.

54. Shaw, *Beyond the Fields*.

55. Bureau of Labor Statistics, "Union Members Summary," January 21, 2011.

56. E.g., Chun, *Organizing at the Margins*, 83–90; Milkman, *L.A. Story*; Kim Voss and Rachel Sherman, "Breaking the Iron Law of Oligarchy: Union Revitalization in the American Labor Movement," *American Journal of Sociology* 106:2 (2000): 303–49.

57. Steve Early, "Membership-Based Organizing," in *A New Labor Movement for the New Century*, ed. Gregory Mantsios (New York: Monthly Review Press, 1998); Bill Fletcher Jr. and Fernando Gapasin, *Solidarity Divided: The Crisis in Organized Labor and a New Path toward Social Justice* (Berkeley: University of California Press, 2008), 65; Cal Winslow, *Labor's Civil War in California: The NUHW Healthcare Workers' Rebellion* (Oakland, Ca.: PM Press, 2010).

58. Steve Early, *The Civil Wars in U.S. Labor: Birth of a New Workers' Movement or Death Throes of the Old?* (Chicago: Haymarket Books, 2011); Fletcher and Gapasin, *Solidarity Divided*; Getman, *Restoring the Power of Unions*, chap. 13; Winslow, *Labor's Civil War in California*.

59. See Steve Early, "Commentary: The Progressive Quandary about SEIU: A Tale of Two Letters to Andy Stern," *WorkingUSA: The Journal of Labor and Society* 12 (2009): 611–28.

60. Milkman, *L.A. Story*, 21–22; Teresa Sharpe, "Union Democracy and Successful Campaigns: The Dynamics of Staff Authority and Worker Participation in an Organizing Union," in *Rebuilding Labor: Organizing and Organizers in the New Union Movement*, ed. Ruth Milkman and Kim Voss, 62–87 (Ithaca: Cornell University Press, 2004); Eve Weinbaum and Gordon Lafer, "Outside Agitators and Other Red Herrings: Getting Past the 'Top-Down/Bottom-Up' Debate," *New Labor Forum* 10 (2002): 26–35.

61. Ganz, "Resources and Resourcefulness"; Getman, *Restoring the Power of Unions*, 317–19.

62. Clawson, *Next Upsurge*, 31.

63. Gramsci, *Prison Notebooks*, 126.

1. The Labor of Love

1. Brad Geagley, *A Compassionate Presence: The Story of the Sisters of St. Joseph of Orange* (Orange, Calif.: Sisters of St. Joseph of Orange, 1987); Barbra Mann Wall, *Unlikely Entrepreneurs: Catholic Sisters and the Hospital Marketplace, 1865–1925* (Columbus: Ohio State University Press, 2005), 23.

2. Wall, *Unlikely Entrepreneurs,* 9.

3. Nelson, *Say Little, Do Much,* 18–19.

4. Christopher Kauffman, *Ministry and Meaning: A Religious History of Catholic Health Care in the United States* (New York: Crossroad, 1995).

5. Nelson, *Say Little, Do Much,* 152.

6. Ibid., 55, 153.

7. Wall, *Unlikely Entrepreneurs,* 51.

8. Nelson, *Say Little, Do Much,* 24–25; Wall, *Unlikely Entrepreneurs,* 8, 17.

9. Geagley, *Compassionate Presence,* 112.

10. Ibid., 113.

11. Wall, *Unlikely Entrepreneurs,* 130, 134.

12. Nelson, *Say Little, Do Much,* 55.

13. Helen Rose Ebaugh, Jon Lorence, and Janet Saltzman Chafetz, "The Growth and Decline of the Population of Catholic Nuns Cross-Nationally, 1960–1990: A Case of Secularization as Social Structural Change," *Journal for the Scientific Study of Religion* 35:2 (1996): 171–83; Margaret Thompson, "Discovering Foremothers: Sisters, Society, and the American Catholic Experience," *U.S. Catholic Historian* 5 (1986): 273–90; Wall, *Unlikely Entrepreneurs,* 35.

14. Nelson, *Say Little, Do Much,* 13.

15. Wall, *Unlikely Entrepreneurs,* 42.

16. Ibid., 116.

17. Stevens, *In Sickness and in Wealth,* chap. 6.

18. Wall, *Unlikely Entrepreneurs,* 43.

19. Thompson, "Discovering Foremothers."

20. Wall, *Unlikely Entrepreneurs,* 120.

21. Johnston, *Success While Others Fail,* 124.

22. Linda Aiken, Robert Blendon, and David Rogers, "The Shortage of Hospital Nurses: A New Perspective," *Annals of Internal Medicine* 95:3 (1981): 365–72.

23. Geagley, *Compassionate Presence,* 220.

24. Ibid., 234.

25. Ibid., 235.

26. Ibid., 248.

27. Ibid., 253.

28. Laurie Goodstein, "New Nuns and Priests Seen Opting for Tradition," *New York Times* (August 10, 2009), A12.

29. Barbra Mann Wall, *American Catholic Hospitals: A Century of Changing Markets and Missions* (New Brunswick, N.J.: Rutgers University Press, 2011), 3.

30. Wall, *American Catholic Hospitals,* chap. 2.

31. Ibid., 4.

32. Scott et al., *Institutional Change and Healthcare Organizations.*

33. Hochschild, *Managed Heart.*

34. Ken Blanchard and Barbara Glanz, *The Simple Truths of Service* (New York: Blanchard Family Partnership, 2005).

35. Wall, *Unlikely Entrepreneurs,* 193. The Sisters of St. Joseph of Carondelet is another order of sisters that traces its origins to Le Puy, France.

36. Raymond Decker, "Position Paper for the Divesting of the Medical Facilities Owned by the Sisters of St. Joseph of Orange." Undated white paper. In author's files.

2. Losing It

1. Soon after this initial meeting, on January 1, 2005, Local 250 would merge with Local 399 to form United Healthcare Workers West (SEIU-UHW).

2. 1199NW, founded in 1983, began as an offshoot of New York City's 1199 healthcare workers' union. Along with other 1199 locals around the country, 1199NW went on to become affiliated with SEIU.

3. Between 1997 and 2002, SEIU led a successful campaign for election ground rules within hospitals owned by Catholic Healthcare West (CHW), the largest not-for-profit hospital system in California and one of the largest Catholic hospital systems in the country.

4. Lopez, *Reorganizing the Rust Belt,* 55–58.

5. Albert Hirschman, *Exit, Voice, and Loyalty: Responses to Decline in Firms, Organizations, and States* (Cambridge: Harvard University Press, 1970).

6. Richard Freeman and James Medoff, *What Do Unions Do?* (New York: Basic Books, 1984).

7. This argument finds mixed support in the literature. See Henry Farber, "Nonunion Wage Rates and the Threat of Unionization," *Industrial and Labor Relations Review* 58:3:2 (2005): 335–52.

8. Bureau of Labor Statistics, "Occupational Employment Statistics: Occupational Employment and Wages," May 2009.

9. Joan Pynes, "The Anticipated Growth of Nonprofit Unionism," *Nonprofit Management and Leadership* 7:4 (1997): 355–71.

10. Jeanne Peters and Jan Masaoka, "A House Divided: How Nonprofits Experience Union Drives," *Nonprofit Management and Leadership* 10:3 (2000): 305–17.

11. Tina Maragou Hovekamp, "Work Values among Professional Employees in Union and Nonunion Research Library Institutions," *Journal of Applied Social Psychology* 24:11 (1994): 981–93; Allen Ponak, "Unionized Professionals and the Scope of Bargaining," *Industrial and Labor Relations Review* 34:3 (1981): 396–407.

12. Barry Hirsch and Edward Schumacher, "Union Wages, Rents, and Skills in Health Care Labor Markets," *Journal of Labor Research* 19:1 (1998): 125–47.

13. Dorothy Sue Cobble, *Dishing It Out: Waitresses and Their Unions in the Twentieth Century* (Urbana: University of Illinois Press, 1991); Fletcher and Gapasin, *Solidarity Divided*, 135.

14. According to the organization's website, approximately 86,000 healthcare workers are members of CNA, which merged in 2009 with other local nursing unions to form the 150,000-member National Nurses United (NNU).

15. Bureau of Labor Statistics, "Career Guide to Industries, 2010–11 Edition: Healthcare," http://www.bls.gov/oco/cg/cgs035.htm.

16. Michael Hannan and John Freeman, "The Ecology of Organizational Mortality: American Labor Unions, 1836–1985," *American Journal of Sociology* 94:1 (1988): 49.

17. Judith Stepan-Norris and Caleb Southworth, "Rival Unionism and Membership Growth: A Special Case of Inter-Organizational Competition," *American Sociological Review* 75:2 (2010): 231.

18. SEIU-UHW Fair Election Commission, "A Report on Workers' Right to Organize at Santa Rosa Memorial Hospital, St. Joseph Health System," (Oakland, Ca: SEIU-UHW, 2005), 9.

19. Ibid., 10, 12, 14, 15, 17–18.

20. Ibid., 20.

21. Ibid., 20, 23.

22. Ibid., 12.

23. A copy of the slideshow is contained in Eileen Purcell's report on the campaign, "St. Joseph Health System Workers' Organizing Campaign," 2009. In author's files.

24. SEIU-UHW was formed in 2004 as a result of a merger between SEIU's two largest California health care unions, SEIU Local 250 and SEIU Local 399.

25. Kate Bronfenbrenner and Tom Juravich, "The Impact of Employer Opposition on Union Certification Win Rates: A Private/Public Sector Comparison," Working Paper Number 113 (Washington, D.C.: Economic Policy Institute, 1995); see also Kate Bronfenbrenner, "Employer Behavior in Certification Elections and First Contracts: Implications for Labor Law Reform," in *Restoring the Promise of American Labor Law*, ed. Sheldon Friedman et al., 75–89 (Ithaca, N.Y.: ILR Press, 1994).

26. Laura Cooper, "Authorization Cards and Union Representation Election Outcome: An Empirical Assessment of the Assumptions Underlying the Supreme Court's *Gissel* Decision," *Northwestern University Law Review* 79:1 (1984): 87–141.

27. Thomas A. Kochan et al., *Healing Together: The Labor-Management Partnership at Kaiser Permanente* (Ithaca: Cornell University Press, 2009).

28. "Sutter Strike Notice 11/20/04 Article Talking Points," Santa Rosa Memorial Hospital internal memo.

29. Johnston, *Success While Others Fail*.

30. Mancur Olson Jr., *The Logic of Collective Action: Public Goods and the Theory of Groups* (Cambridge: Harvard University Press, 1971).

31. Fantasia, *Cultures of Solidarity*.

32. For a review, see Getman, *Restoring the Power of Unions*, part 3; Chirag Mehta and Nik Theodore, *Undermining the Right to Organize: Employer Behavior during Union Representation Campaigns* (Washington, D.C.: American Rights at Work, 2005).

33. Gordon Lafer, "Free and Fair? How Labor Law Fails U.S. Democratic Election Standards" (Washington, D.C.: American Rights at Work, 2005), 9.

34. Ibid., 27.

35. Report from forum on organizing rights with St. Joseph Health System, September 29, 2005. In author's files.

36. On September 27, 2007, the advertisement appeared in several large daily newspapers, including the *San Francisco Chronicle*, the *Orange County Register*, the *Santa Rosa Press Democrat*, and the *Los Angeles Times*.

37. Randi Rossmann, "Sutter to Remain in Santa Rosa," *Press Democrat*, March 11, 2008.

38. Johnston, *Success While Others Fail*, 12.

39. Ibid., 11.

40. Ibid., 12.

41. On "political opportunity structure," see Doug McAdam, *Political Process and the Development of Black Insurgency, 1930–1970* (Chicago: University of Chicago Press, 1982), 40.

42. In anticipation of increased traffic as a result of the Sutter deal, Memorial Hospital had announced that it would expand its inpatient capacity by 80 beds, would double the size of its emergency room, and would expand its parking garage. After the deal fell through, many of the beds that were added proved difficult to fill, and the parking garage expansion was scrapped after having been started. The failed deal with Sutter was likely responsible for the abrupt departure of Memorial's CEO, George Perez. Guy Kovner, "Colleagues Say Perez Felt Brunt of Failed Deal," *Santa Rosa Press Democrat*, August 16, 2008.

43. Clawson, *Next Upsurge*, 110–24.

3. A Struggle Over New Things

1. "SEIU Healthcare Division: National Catholic Strategy—Projecting a National Settlement Within Catholic Healthcare," union memorandum, February 7, 2007.

2. Jeffrey Krasner, "Caritas and SEIU Reach Accord: Deal Paves Way for Union Effort," *Boston Globe*, January 27, 2009.

3. Purcell, "Organizing Campaign," 3.

4. Ibid., 3–4.

5. SEIU international union memo in author's files.

6. See, for example, Henry Browne, *The Catholic Church and the Knights of Labor* (Washington, D.C.: Catholic University of America Press, 1949); Douglas Seaton, *Catholics and Radicals: The Association of Catholic Trade Unionists and the American Labor Movement, from Depression to Cold War* (Lewisburg: Bucknell University Press, 1981).

7. Joseph Fahey to Jack Glaser and Kevin Murphy, January 31, 2008. In author's files.

8. Ibid.

9. Monsignor George Higgins, *Organized Labor and the Church: Reflections of a "Labor Priest"* (New York: Paulist Press, 1993).

10. Pontifical Council for Justice and Peace, *Compendium of the Social Doctrine of the Church* (Strathfield, Australia: St. Paul's Publications, 2005), 134.

11. John Glaser, "Fruit on the Diseased Tree of U.S. Healthcare," *Health Care Ethics* 15:1 (2007), 2–4.

12. John Glaser, "'Covering the Uninsured' Is a Flawed Moral Frame," *Health Progress* 87:2 (March–April 2006).

13. Arthur Jones, "Center Plans Dialogue on Health Reform," *National Catholic Reporter*, September 10, 2004.

14. Notes from meeting between Glaser and union representatives, September 6, 2005. In author's files.

15. PowerPoint presentation delivered on September 6, 2005. In author's files.

16. Andrew Galvin, "Stalemate at St. Joseph: Union Is Trying to Organize Hospital Workers, but Won't File for an Election until Management First Agrees to Ground Rules," *Orange County Register*, October 31, 2007.

17. Nelson, *Say Little, Do Much*, 54.

18. Patricia Talone, "Labor and Catholic Health Care," *Health Progress*, March–April 2002, 36.

19. Talone, "Labor and Catholic Health Care," 36.

20. Ibid.

21. Report from forum on organizing rights within St. Joseph Health System, September 29, 2005, Santa Rosa, California. In author's files.

22. Purcell, "Organizing Campaign," 3.

23. Ibid.

24. Ibid., 2.

25. Summary of meeting between Sister Katherine Gray, Deborah Proctor, and Robert Reich, February 27, 2007, Orange, California. In author's files.

26. In an NLRB case documented by James Gross (1995); see also Clawson, *Next Upsurge*), every worker at Blue Flash Company had signed union cards and then denied having done so when questioned in mandatory meetings with supervisors.

27. Suzanne Gordon, "Unions—Unfair to Workers?" *Mother Jones* (April–May 1986), 14–18.

28. Gordon, "Unions—Unfair to Workers?" 14.

29. Lance Compa, *Unfair Advantage: Workers' Freedom of Association in the United States under International Human Rights Standards* (New York: Human Rights Watch, 2000).

30. Ganz, "Resources and Resourcefulness"; Sharpe, "Union Democracy and Successful Campaigns"; Voss and Sherman, "Breaking the Iron Law of Oligarchy"; Weinbaum and Lafer, "Outside Agitators and Other Red Herrings."

31. Sharpe, "Union Democracy and Successful Campaigns."

32. Rick Fantasia and Kim Voss, *Hard Work: Remaking the American Labor Movement* (Berkeley: University of California Press, 2004), 126–34; Getman, *Restoring the Power of Unions*, chap. 10; Milkman, *L.A. Story*.

33. Carol Benfell, "Union Vote Sought at Memorial: SEIU to Ask for Agreement on Ground Rules, but SR Hospital Officials Say It's Unnecessary," *Santa Rosa Press Democrat*, July 12, 2006.

34. Summary of meeting between Sister Katherine Gray, Deborah Proctor, and Robert Reich, February 27, 2007, Orange, California.

35. Monsignor John Brenkle, "Catholic Diocese Disagrees with Memorial's Position on Union," *Santa Rosa Press Democrat*, May 11, 2007.

36. Purcell, "Organizing Campaign," 26.

37. Jarol Manheim, *Trends in Union Corporate Campaigns* (Washington, D.C.: United States Chamber of Commerce, 2005), 16.

38. Ibid., 23

39. Manheim, *Death of a Thousand Cuts*, xiv.

40. Notes from meeting between Glaser and union representatives, September 6, 2005. From Eileen Purcell files.

41. Randy Shaw, "Palin Not Alone in Bashing Community Organizers," *BeyondChron.org*, September 11, 2008.

42. "Editorial: St. Joseph Dispute Is Not about Justice," *Orange County Register*, August 10, 2008.

43. Notes from meeting between Glaser and union representatives, September 6, 2005. In author's files.

44. Notes on e-mail correspondence between Fahey and Glaser. In author's files.

4. Winning the Heart Way

1. John Van der Zee, "Agony in the Garden: A California Diocese Recovers from a Sex-Abuse Scandal, and Finds That Healing Comes through Facing the Truth," *Salon.com*, March 30, 2000.

2. Mark Granovetter, *Getting a Job: A Study of Contacts and Careers* (Cambridge, Mass.: Harvard University Press, 1974); Robert Putnam, *Bowling Alone: The Collapse and Revival of American Community* (New York: Simon and Schuster, 2000); William Julius Wilson, *The Truly Disadvantaged: The Inner City, the Underclass, and Public Policy* (Chicago: University of Chicago Press, 1987); Michael Useem, *The Inner Circle: Large Corporations and the Rise of Business Political Activity in the US and UK* (New York: Oxford University Press, 1984); Brian Uzzi, "The Sources and Consequences of Embeddedness for the Economic Performance of Organizations: The Network Effect," *American Journal of Sociology* 61:4 (1996): 674–98; Ganz, "Resources and Resourcefulness"; Roger Gould, "Collective Action and Network Structure," *American Sociological Review* 58:2 (1993): 182–96.

3. Albert Hirschman, "Against Parsimony: Three Easy Ways of Complicating Some Categories of Economic Discourse," *American Economic Review* 74:2 (1984): 89–96.

4. Purcell, "Organizing Campaign," 37.

5. IAF did support the union in other ways. For example, IAF organizers did help union leaders secure meetings with some significant religious leaders in Southern California during the campaign.

6. For an extensive description of the IAF model, see Mark Warren, *Dry Bones Rattling: Community Building to Revitalize America's Democracy* (Princeton: Princeton University Press, 2001).

7. Purcell, "St. Joseph Health System Organizing Campaign," 40.

8. For a review, see Francesca Polletta, "Storytelling in Social Movements," in *Culture, Social Movements, and Protest*, ed. Hank Johnston (Burlington, Vt.: Ashgate, 2009).

9. Purcell, "Organizing Campaign," 43.

10. Ibid., 15.

11. Ibid., 42.

12. Ibid.

13. Shaw, *Beyond the Fields*, 87.

14. Eileen Purcell, "United States Conference (USCCB) Domestic Policy Sub Committee on Catholic Healthcare: A Brief History" (February 2007). In author's files.

15. For example, Peter Steinfels, "Catholic Health Organizations and Labor Unions Try to Bridge Gap," *New York Times*, September 4, 1999; "Bishops' Committee Seeks Healing for Labor, Healthcare Relations," *Catholic Health World*, September 12, 1999.

16. Purcell, "United States Conference (USCCB) Domestic Policy Sub Committee on Catholic Healthcare."

17. Brenkle, "Catholic Diocese Disagrees with Memorial's Position on Union," *Santa Rosa Press Democrat*, May 11, 2007.

18. Victoria Colliver, "Labor Dispute Divides Religious Community: Priests Back Workers at Hospital Chain Run by Order of Nuns," *San Francisco Chronicle*, January 27, 2008.

19. Rosemary Radford Ruether, "The Sisters, the Workers, and the Union," *National Catholic Reporter*, October 19, 2007.

20. Eileen Purcell notes.

21. Daffodil Altan, "A Union Busting Habit: The Sisters Who Run St. Joseph Health System Are Often Pro-Labor—But Apparently Not at Their Hospitals," *OC Weekly*, August 16, 2007; Daffodil Altan, "Sister Knows Best! If the Nuns in Charge of the St. Joseph Health System Are So Pro-Labor, Why Are Some of Their Employees Determined to Unionize?" *OC Weekly*, November 30, 2007.

22. Andrew Galvin, "Stalemate at St. Joseph: Union Is Trying to Organize Hospital Workers, but Won't File for an Election until Management First Agrees to Ground Rules," *Orange County Register*, October 31, 2007; Yvette Cabrera, "Hospital Workers Want Their Voices Heard," *Orange County Register*, June 17, 2008.

23. Fax sent to Eileen Purcell on January 10, 2007: "SJHS Code of Conduct for Third Party Representation Discussions." In author's files.

24. According to international leaders, several other SEIU campaigns in religious hospital systems had failed or been put on hold, including one at Catholic Health Services of Long Island (CHSLI) and ones within Advocate Health Care in Chicago, Providence Health System in Seattle and Southern California, and Catholic Health Partners in Ohio.

5. Trouble in the House of Labor

1. Ganz, *Why David Sometimes Wins*, 239.

2. Adam Przeworski, *Capitalism and Social Democracy* (Cambridge: Cambridge University Press, 1985).

3. Ibid., 24.

4. Winslow, *Labor's Civil War in California*, 39–41.

5. Przeworski, *Capitalism and Social Democracy*, 27.

6. Michael Rose, "Workers in 39 of 44 Units at Hospitals, Homes in Ohio Reject Representation by SEIU," *Labor Relations Week* (January 21, 2011).

7. Voss and Sherman, "Breaking the Iron Law of Oligarchy."

8. Fletcher and Gapasin, *Solidarity Divided*, 65; Early, *Civil Wars in U.S. Labor*.

9. Milkman, *L.A. Story*.

10. Fletcher and Gapasin, *Solidarity Divided*, 128; Winslow, *Labor's Civil War in California*, 36–37.

11. "Interview with Sal Rosselli, Leader of National Union of Healthcare Workers," *Fight Back! News*, May 20, 2010.

12. Clawson, *The Next Upsurge*, 45–46; Fletcher and Gapasin, *Solidarity Divided*, 124; Winslow, *Labor's Civil War in California*, 44.

13. Getman, *Restoring the Power of Unions*, chap. 13.

14. Ibid., 146.

15. Forty nursing homes ultimately were organized.

16. Given the precarious financial position of many nursing home companies, lawsuits against them often lead to bankruptcy, meaning that the business is then sold to another company without the underlying problems being addressed. Moreover, liability insurance—according to some experts—could be better spent on improving patient care: R. Patrick Bedell. "The Next Frontier in Tort Reform: Promoting the Financial Solvency of Nursing Homes," *Elder Law Journal* 11:2 (2003): 361–65; David Stevenson and David Studdert, "The Rise of Nursing Home Litigation: Findings from a National Survey of Attorneys," *Health Affairs* 22:2 (2003): 219–29; David Studdert and David Stevenson, "Nursing Home Litigation and Tort Reform: A Case for 'Exceptionalism.'" *Gerontologist* 44:5 (2004): 588–95.

17. Matt Smith, "Partners in Slime: The California Employees' Union and the Nursing Home Industry Join Forces to Increase Profit, Grow Union Membership, and Sell Out Abused Nursing Home Patients," *San Francisco Weekly*, June 30, 2004.

18. Matt Smith, "Union Disunity: The Secret Deal Worked Out between SEIU Bosses and the Nursing Home Owners Denies Union Members the Right to Speak Out, Strike, or Protect Patients," *San Francisco Weekly*, April 11, 2007.

19. Steven Greenhouse, "Rival Unions Battle in Ohio over Workers at Hospitals," *New York Times*, March 12, 2008.

20. Steven Greenhouse, "An Internal Dispute Turns Nasty, with a Local in the Balance," *New York Times*, January 17, 2009.

21. Paul Pringle, "Leader's Kin Get Union Business," *Los Angeles Times*, August 9, 2008.

22. Steven Greenhouse, "An Internal Dispute Turns Nasty, with a Local in the Balance," *New York Times*, January 17, 2009.

23. Steven Greenhouse, "A Union President Presses for Growth amid a New Round of Criticisms," *New York Times*, June 1, 2008.

24. Steven Greenhouse, "Trustee May Take Helm of Union Local in Dispute," *New York Times*, January 22, 2009.

25. Ibid.

26. From www.nuhw.org.

27. Martin Espinoza, "Memorial Hospital to Lay Off 152; Petaluma Valley to Trim 30 jobs," *Santa Rosa Press Democrat*, February 4, 2009.

28. D. Ashley Furness, "Memorial Hospital Election Set after Long Union Battle," *North Bay Business Journal*, November 9, 2009.

29. Randy Shaw, "Is Fresno SEIU's Vietnam?" *BeyondChron.com*, June 22, 2009.

30. United States of America before the National Labor Relations Board Division of Judges San Francisco Branch Office, 20-RC-18241 (May 28, 2010).

31. Martin J. Bennett, "Memorial Hospital and Right to Organize," *Santa Rosa Press Democrat*, December 21, 2010; Compa, *Unfair Advantage*; Samuel Estreicher and Matthew T. Bodie, "Review Essay—Administrative Delay at the NLRB: Some Modest Proposals," *Journal of Labor Research* 23:1 (2002): 87–104.

Conclusion

1. Freeman and Medoff, *What Do Unions Do?*

2. Freeman and Medoff, *What Do Unions Do?*; John Kwoka, "Monopoly, Plant, and Union Effects on Worker Wages," *Industrial and Labor Relations Review* 36 (1983): 251–57; Beth A. Rubin, "Class Struggle American Style: Unions, Strikes and Wages," *American Sociological Review* 51 (1986): 618–33; Bruce Western, *Between Class and Market: Postwar Unionization in the Capitalist Democracies* (Princeton: Princeton University Press, 1997).

3. Hirsch and Macpherson, *Union Membership and Earnings Data Book*.

4. Thomas Buchmueller, John DiNardo, and Robert Valletta, "Union Effects on Health Insurance Provision and Coverage in the United States," Working Paper No. 8238 (Cambridge: National Bureau of Economic Research, 2001).

5. Richard Freeman, "The Exit-Voice Tradeoff in the Labor Market: Unionism, Job Tenure, Quits, and Separations," *Quarterly Journal of Economics* 94 (1980): 643–73.

6. Gordon, *Nursing against the Odds*, 292.

7. Freeman and Rogers, *What Workers Want*; Barry Hirsch, J. Michael DuMond, and David Macpherson, "Workers' Compensation Recipiency in Union and Nonunion Workplaces," *Industrial and Labor Relations Review* 50:2 (1997): 213–36.

8. Brian Becker, "Hospital Unionism and Employment Stability," *Industrial Relations* 17:1 (1978): 96–101; Lawrence Kahn and Kimio Morimune, "Unions and Employment Stability: A Sequential Logit Approach," *International Economic Review* 20:1 (1979): 217–35; Freeman, "Exit-Voice Tradeoff"; James Medoff, "Layoffs and Alternatives under Trade Unions in U.S. Manufacturing," *American Economic Review* 69:3 (1979): 380–95; Solomon Polachek and Ernest McCutcheon, "Union Effects on Employment Stability: A Comparison of Panel versus Cross-Sectional Data," *Journal of Labor Research* 4:3 (1983): 273–87. Despite consistently positive estimations of the relationships between unionization and wages, and unionization and job stability, many have raised questions about standard cross-sectional OLS analyses, arguing that union membership is likely endogenous to omitted variables such as worker skill or productivity: H. Gregg Lewis, *Union Relative Wage Effects: A Survey* (Chicago: University of Chicago Press, 1986); Polachek and McCutcheon, "Union Effects." Nevertheless, Chris Robinson has conducted some of the most comprehensive comparisons of different modeling techniques for addressing the endogeneity problem regarding the wage premium, and concluded that OLS cross-sectional data may actually *understate* the wage premium: Chris Robinson, "The Joint Determination of Union

Status and Union Wage Effects: Some Tests of Alternative Methods," *Journal of Political Economy* 97:3 (1989): 639–67.

9. Burawoy, *Manufacturing Consent,* 18.

10. Clawson, *Next Upsurge,* 194.

11. For exceptions, see Ash and Seago, "The Effect of Registered Nurses' Unions on Heart-Attack Mortality"; Gordon, *Safety in Numbers.*

12. Kochan et al., *Healing Together,* 22–23.

13. Ibid.

14. Chun, *Organizing at the Margins.*

15. Fletcher and Gapasin, *Solidarity Divided,* 128.

16. Andy Stern, *A Country That Works: Getting America Back on Track* (New York: Free Press, 2006), 15.

17. Voss and Sherman, "Breaking the Iron Law of Oligarchy."

18. Robert Michels, *Political Parties: A Sociological Study of the Oligarchical Tendencies of Modern Democracy* (New York: Free Press, 1962).

19. Bureau of Labor Statistics, "Career Guide to Industries, 2010–2011 Edition: Healthcare," http://www.bls.gov/oco/cg/cgs035.htm#related.

20. Milkman, *L.A. Story,* 152.

21. Fletcher and Gapasin, *Solidarity Divided,* 207.

22. Ibid., 206.

23. Ganz, "Resources and Resourcefulness."

BIBLIOGRAPHY

Aiken, Linda H., Robert J. Blendon, and David E. Rogers. "The Shortage of Hospital Nurses: A New Perspective." *Annals of Internal Medicine* 95:3 (1981): 365–72.

Ash, Michael, and Jean Ann Seago. "The Effect of Registered Nurses' Unions on Heart-Attack Mortality." *Industrial and Labor Relations Review* 57:3 (2004): 422–42.

Becker, Brian. "Hospital Unionism and Employment Stability." *Industrial Relations* 17:1 (1978): 96–101.

Bedell, R. Patrick. "The Next Frontier in Tort Reform: Promoting the Financial Solvency of Nursing Homes." *Elder Law Journal* 11:2 (2003): 361–65.

Blanchflower, David G., and Alex Bryson. "What Effect Do Unions Have on Wages Now and Would Freeman and Medoff Be Surprised?" *Journal of Labor Research* 15:3 (2004): 383–414.

Blau, Peter M. *Exchange and Power in Social Life*. New York: John Wiley and Sons, 1964.

Bratsberg, Bernt, and James F. Ragan Jr. "Changes in the Union Wage Premium by Industry." *Industrial and Labor Relations Review* 56:1 (2002): 65–83.

Bronfenbrenner, Kate. "Employer Behavior in Certification Elections and First Contracts: Implications for Labor Law Reform." In *Restoring the Promise of American Labor Law*, edited by Sheldon Friedman, Richard W. Hurd, Rudolph A. Oswald, and Ronald L. Seeber, 75–89. Ithaca, N.Y.: ILR Press, 1994.

Bronfenbrenner, Kate, and Tom Juravich. "It Takes More Than House Calls: Organizing to Win with a Comprehensive Union-Building Strategy." In *Organizing to Win: New Research on Union Strategies*, edited by Kate Bronfenbrenner, Sheldon Friedman, Richard W. Hurd, Rudolph A. Oswald, and Ronald L. Seeber, 19–36. Ithaca, N.Y.: ILR Press, 1998.

———. "The Impact of Employer Opposition on Union Certification Win Rates: A Private/Public Sector Comparison." Working Paper Number 113. Washington, D.C.: Economic Policy Institute, 1995.

Browne, Henry J. *The Catholic Church and the Knights of Labor*. Washington, D.C.: Catholic University of America Press, 1949.

Bryan-Brown, Christopher, and Kathleen Dracup. "Professionalism." *American Journal of Critical Care* 12 (2003): 394–96.

Buchmueller, Thomas C., John DiNardo, and Robert G. Valletta. "Union Effects on Health Insurance Provision and Coverage in the United States." Working Paper No. 8238. Cambridge: National Bureau of Economic Research, 2001.

Budrys, Grace. *When Doctors Join Unions*. Ithaca, N.Y.: ILR Press, 1997.

Burawoy, Michael. *Manufacturing Consent: Changes in the Labor Process under Monopoly Capitalism*. Chicago: University of Chicago Press, 1979.

———. *The Politics of Production: Factory Regimes under Capitalism and Socialism*. London: Verso, 1985.

Catholic Health Association of the United States. "Catholic Health Care in the United States." Washington, D.C., 2011.

Chun, Jennifer Jihye. *Organizing at the Margins: The Symbolic Politics of Labor in South Korea and the United States*. Ithaca, N.Y.: Cornell University Press, 2009.

Clawson, Dan. *The Next Upsurge: Labor and the New Social Movements*. Ithaca, N.Y.: Cornell University Press, 2003.

Cobble, Dorothy Sue. *Dishing It Out: Waitresses and Their Unions in the Twentieth Century*. Urbana: University of Illinois Press, 1991.

Cohen, Larry, and Richard W. Hurd. "Fear, Conflict, and Union Organizing." In *Organizing to Win: New Research on Union Strategies*, edited by Kate Bronfenbrenner, Sheldon Friedman, Richard W. Hurd, Rudolph A. Oswald, and Ronald L. Seeber, 181–96. Ithaca, N.Y.: ILR Press, 1998.

Compa, Lance. *Unfair Advantage: Workers' Freedom of Association in the United States under International Human Rights Standards*. New York: Human Rights Watch, 2000.

Cooper, Laura. "Authorization Cards and Union Representation Election Outcome: An Empirical Assessment of the Assumptions Underlying the Supreme Court's *Gissel* Decision." *Northwestern University Law Review* 79:1 (1984): 87–141.

Decker, Raymond. "Position Paper for the Divesting of the Medical Facilities Owned by the Sisters of St. Joseph of Orange." Undated white paper. In author's files.

Early, Steve. "Membership-Based Organizing." In *A New Labor Movement for the New Century*, edited by Gregory Mantsios, 82–103. New York: Monthly Review Press, 1998.

———. "Commentary: The Progressive Quandary about SEIU: A Tale of Two Letters to Andy Stern." *WorkingUSA: The Journal of Labor and Society* 12:4 (2009): 611–28.

———. *The Civil Wars in U.S. Labor: Birth of a New Workers' Movement or Death Throes of the Old?* Chicago: Haymarket Books, 2011.

Ebaugh, Helen Rose, Jon Lorence, and Janet Saltzman Chafetz. "The Growth and Decline of the Population of Catholic Nuns Cross-Nationally, 1960–1990: A Case of Secularization as Social Structural Change." *Journal for the Scientific Study of Religion* 35:2 (1996): 171–83.

Ehrenreich, Barbara, and John Ehrenreich. "Hospital Workers: Class Conflicts in the Making." *International Journal of Health Services* 5:1 (1975): 43–51.

England, Paula, Michelle Budig, and Nancy Folbre. "Wages of Virtue: The Relative Pay of Care Work." *Social Problems* 49:4 (2002): 455–73.

Estreicher, Samuel, and Matthew T. Bodie. "Review Essay—Administrative Delay at the NLRB: Some Modest Proposals." *Journal of Labor Research* 23:1 (2002) 87–104.

Fantasia, Rick. *Cultures of Solidarity: Consciousness, Action, and Contemporary American Workers*. Berkeley: University of California Press, 1988.

Fantasia, Rick, and Kim Voss. *Hard Work: Remaking the American Labor Movement*. Berkeley: University of California Press, 2004.

Farber, Henry. "Nonunion Wage Rates and the Threat of Unionization." *Industrial and Labor Relations Review* 58:3:2 (2005): 335–52.

Fink, Leon, and Brian Greenberg. *Upheaval in the Quiet Zone: A History of Hospital Workers' Union, Local 1199*. Chicago: University of Illinois Press, 1989.

Fletcher, Bill, Jr., and Fernando Gapasin, *Solidarity Divided: The Crisis in Organized Labor and a New Path toward Social Justice*. Berkeley: University of California Press, 2008.

Freeman, Richard B. "The Exit-Voice Tradeoff in the Labor Market: Unionism, Job Tenure, Quits, and Separations." *Quarterly Journal of Economics* 94:4 (1980): 643–73.

———. "Longitudinal Analyses of the Effects of Trade Unions." *Journal of Labor Economics* 2:1 (1984): 1–26.

Freeman, Richard B., and James L. Medoff. *What Do Unions Do?* New York: Basic Books, 1984.

Freeman, Richard B., and Joel Rogers. *What Workers Want*. Ithaca, N.Y.: Cornell University Press, 1999.

Ganz, Marshall. "Resources and Resourcefulness: Strategic Capacity in the Unionization of California Agriculture, 1959–1966." *American Journal of Sociology* 105:4 (2000): 1003–62.

———. *Why David Sometimes Wins: Leadership, Organization, and Strategy in the California Farm Worker Movement*. New York: Oxford University Press, 2009.

Geagley, Brad. *A Compassionate Presence: The Story of the Sisters of St. Joseph of Orange*. Orange, Calif.: Sisters of St. Joseph of Orange, 1987.

Gersick, Connie J. G. "Pacing Strategic Change: The Case of a New Venture." *Academy of Management Journal* 37:1 (1994): 9–45.

Getman, Julius G. *Restoring the Power of Unions: It Takes a Movement*. New Haven: Yale University Press, 2010.

Glaser, John W. "Catholic Health Ministry: Fruit on the Diseased Tree of U.S. Health Care." *Health Care Ethics U.S.A.* 15:1 (2007): 2–4.

Gordon, Suzanne. *Nursing against the Odds: How Health Care Cost Cutting, Media Stereotypes, and Medical Hubris Undermine Nurses and Patient Care*. Ithaca, N.Y.: Cornell University Press, 2005.

———. "Unions—Unfair to Workers?" *Mother Jones* (April–May 1986): 14–18.

Gordon, Suzanne, John Buchanan, and Tanya Bretherton. *Safety in Numbers: Nurse-to-Patient Ratios and the Future of Healthcare.* Ithaca, N.Y.: Cornell University Press, 2008.

Gould, Roger V. "Collective Action and Network Structure." *American Sociological Review*, 58:2 (1993): 182–96.

Gramsci, Antonio. *Further Selections from the Prison Notebooks.* Translated and edited by Derek Boothman. Minneapolis: University of Minnesota Press, 1995.

Granovetter, Mark. *Getting a Job: A Study of Contacts and Careers.* Cambridge, Mass.: Harvard University Press, 1974.

Gross, James A. *Broken Promise: The Subversion of U.S. Labor Relations Policy, 1947–1994.* Philadelphia: Temple University Press, 1995.

Hannan, Michael T., and John Freeman. "The Ecology of Organizational Mortality: American Labor Unions, 1836–1985." *American Journal of Sociology* 94:1 (1988): 25–52.

Higgins, Monsignor George G., with William Bole. *Organized Labor and the Church: Reflections of a "Labor Priest."* New York: Paulist Press, 1993.

Hirsch, Barry T., David A. Macpherson, and J. Michael DuMond. "Worker's Compensation Recipiency in Union and Nonunion Workplaces." *Industrial and Labor Relations Review* 50:2 (1997): 213–36.

Hirsch, Barry T., and David A. Macpherson. *Union Membership and Earnings Databook: Compilations from the Current Population Survey.* Arlington, Va.: Bureau of National Affairs, 2010.

Hirsch, Barry, and Edward J. Schumacher. "Private Sector Union Density and the Wage Premium: Past, Present, and Future." *Journal of Labor Research* 22:3 (2001): 487–518.

———. "Union Wages, Rents, and Skills in Health Care Labor Markets." *Journal of Labor Research* 19:1 (1998): 125–47.

Hirschman, Albert O. "Against Parsimony: Three Easy Ways of Complicating Some Categories of Economic Discourse." *American Economic Review* 74:2 (1984): 89–96.

———. *Exit, Voice, and Loyalty: Responses to Decline in Firms, Organizations, and States.* Cambridge, Mass.: Harvard University Press, 1970.

Hochschild, Arlie R. *The Managed Heart: Commercialization of Human Feeling.* Berkeley: University of California, 1983.

Hoerr, John P. *We Can't Eat Prestige: The Women Who Organized Harvard.* Philadelphia: Temple University Press, 1997.

Hondagneu-Sotelo, Pierrette. *God's Heart Has No Borders: How Religious Activists Are Working for Immigrant Rights.* Berkeley: University of California Press, 2008.

Hovekamp, Tina Maragou. "Work Values among Professional Employees in Union and Nonunion Research Library Institutions." *Journal of Applied Social Psychology* 24:11 (1994): 981–93.

Hughes, Charles. *Making Unions Unnecessary.* New York: Executive Enterprises Publications, 1976.

Jacoby, Sanford M. *Employing Bureaucracy: Managers, Unions, and the Transformation of Work in American Industry, 1900–1945.* New York: Columbia University Press, 1985.

——, ed. *Masters to Managers: Historical and Comparative Perspectives on American Employers*. New York: Columbia University Press, 1991.

Johnston, Paul. *Success While Others Fail: Social Movement Unionism and the Public Workplace*. Ithaca, N.Y.: ILR Press, 1994.

Kahn, Lawrence M., and Kimio Morimune. "Unions and Employment Stability: A Sequential Logit Approach." *International Economic Review* 20:1 (1979): 217–35.

Kauffman, Christopher J. "Catholic Health Care in the United States: American Pluralism and Religious Meanings." *Christian Bioethics* 5:1 (1999): 44–65.

——. *Ministry and Meaning: A Religious History of Catholic Health Care in the United States*. New York: Crossroad, 1995.

Kochan, Thomas A., Adrienne E. Eaton, Robert B. McKersie, and Paul S. Adler. *Healing Together: The Labor-Management Partnership at Kaiser Permanente*. Ithaca, N.Y.: Cornell University Press, 2009.

Kochan, Thomas A., Harry C. Katz, and Robert B. McKersie. *The Transformation of American Industrial Relations*. New York: Basic Books, 1986.

Kwoka, John E. "Monopoly, Plant, and Union Effects on Worker Wages." *Industrial and Labor Relations Review* 36:2 (1983): 251–57.

Lafer, Gordon. "Free and Fair? How Labor Law Fails U.S. Democratic Election Standards." Washington, D.C.: American Rights at Work, 2005.

Lewis, H. Gregg. *Union Relative Wage Effects: A Survey*. Chicago: University of Chicago Press, 1986.

Logan, John. "The Union Avoidance Industry in the United States." *British Journal of Industrial Relations* 44:4 (2006): 651–75.

Lopez, Steven Henry. "Emotional Labor and Organized Emotional Care: Conceptualizing Nursing Home Care Work." *Work and Occupations* 33:2 (2006): 133–60.

——. *Reorganizing the Rust Belt: An Inside Study of the American Labor Movement*. Berkeley: University of California Press, 2004.

Manheim, Jarol B. *The Death of a Thousand Cuts: Corporate Campaigns and the Attack on the Corporation*. New York: Routledge, 2000.

——. *Trends in Union Corporate Campaigns*. Washington, D.C.: United States Chamber of Commerce, 2005.

McAdam, Doug. *Political Process and the Development of Black Insurgency, 1930–1970*. Chicago: University of Chicago Press, 1982.

McAdam, Doug, John D. McCarthy, and Mayer N. Zald, eds. *Comparative Perspectives on Social Movements: Political Opportunities, Mobilizing Structures, and Cultural Framings*. New York: Cambridge University Press, 1996.

McAdam, Doug, and W. Richard Scott. "Organizations and Movements." In *Social Movements and Organizational Theory*, edited by Gerald F. Davis, Doug McAdam, W. Richard Scott, and Mayer N. Zald, 4–40. New York: Cambridge University Press, 2005.

Medoff, James L. "Layoffs and Alternatives under Trade Unions in U.S. Manufacturing." *American Economic Review* 69:3 (1979): 380–95.

Mehta, Chirag, and Nik Theodore. *Undermining the Right to Organize: Employer Behavior during Union Representation Campaigns*. Washington, D.C.: American Rights at Work, 2005.

Michels, Robert. *Political Parties: A Sociological Study of the Oligarchical Tendencies of Modern Democracy*. New York: Free Press, 1962.

Milkman, Ruth. *L.A. Story: Immigrant Workers and the Future of the U.S. Labor Movement*. New York: Russell Sage Foundation, 2006.

Nelson, Sioban. *Say Little, Do Much: Nursing, Nuns, and Hospitals in the Nineteenth Century*. Philadelphia: University of Pennsylvania Press, 2001.

Olson, Mancur, Jr. *The Logic of Collective Action: Public Goods and the Theory of Groups*. Cambridge, Mass.: Harvard University Press, 1971.

Penney, Robert A. "Interpretation, Meaning, and Worker Solidarity." *Social Problems* 53:2 (2006): 139–60.

Peters, Jeanne B., and Jan Masaoka. "A House Divided: How Nonprofits Experience Union Drives." *Nonprofit Management and Leadership* 10:3 (2000): 305–17.

Pfeffer, Jeffrey, and Gerald R. Salancik. *The External Control of Organizations: A Resource Dependence Perspective*. New York: Harper and Row, 1978.

Polachek, Solomon W., and Ernest P. McCutcheon. "Union Effects on Employment Stability: A Comparison of Panel versus Cross-Sectional Data." *Journal of Labor Research* 4:3 (1983): 273–87.

Polletta, Francesca. "Storytelling in Social Movements." In *Culture, Social Movements, and Protest*, edited by Hank Johnston. Burlington, Vt.: Ashgate, 2009.

Ponak, Allen M. "Unionized Professionals and the Scope of Bargaining." *Industrial and Labor Relations Review* 34:3 (1981): 396–407.

Pontifical Council for Justice and Peace. *Compendium of the Social Doctrine of the Church* Strathfield, Australia: St. Paul's Publications, 2005.

Purcell, Eileen. "St. Joseph Health System Workers' Organizing Campaign." SEIU campaign history. 2009. In author's files.

Putnam, Robert. *Bowling Alone: The Collapse and Revival of American Community*. New York: Simon and Schuster, 2000.

Przeworski, Adam. *Capitalism and Social Democracy*. Cambridge: Cambridge University Press, 1985.

Pynes, Joan E. "The Anticipated Growth of Nonprofit Unionism." *Nonprofit Management and Leadership* 7:4 (1997): 355–71.

Robinson, Chris. "The Joint Determination of Union Status and Union Wage Effects: Some Tests of Alternative Methods." *Journal of Political Economy* 97:3 (1989): 639–67.

Rosenberg, Charles. *The Care of Strangers: The Rise of America's Hospital System*. New York: Basic Books, 1987.

Rubin, Beth A. "Class Struggle American Style: Unions, Strikes and Wages." *American Sociological Review* 51:5 (1986): 618–33.

Rundle, James. "Winning Hearts and Minds in the Era of Employee-Involvement Programs." In *Organizing to Win: New Research on Union Strategies*, edited by Kate Bronfenbrenner, Sheldon Friedman, Richard W. Hurd, Rudolph A. Oswald, and Ronald L. Seeber. 213–31. Ithaca, N.Y.: ILR Press, 1998.

Schmidt, Laura Ann. *The Corporate Transformation of American Healthcare*. Unpublished manuscript. In author's files.

Scott, W. Richard, Martin Ruef, Peter J. Mendel, and Carol A. Caronna. *Institutional Change and Healthcare Organizations: From Professional Dominance to Managed Care*. Chicago: University of Chicago Press, 2000.

Seaton, Douglas P. *Catholics and Radicals: The Association of Catholic Trade Unionists and the American Labor Movement, from Depression to Cold War*. Lewisburg, Pa.: Bucknell University Press, 1980.

SEIU-UHW Fair Election Commission. "A Report on Workers' Right to Organize at Santa Rosa Memorial Hospital, St. Joseph Health System." Oakland, Ca.: SEIU-UHW, 2005.

Sharpe, Teresa. "Union Democracy and Successful Campaigns: The Dynamics of Staff Authority and Worker Participation in an Organizing Union." In *Rebuilding Labor: Organizing and Organizers in the New Union Movement*, edited by Ruth Milkman and Kim Voss, 62–87. Ithaca, N.Y.: Cornell University Press, 2004.

Shaw, Randy. *Beyond the Fields: Cesar Chavez, the UFW, and the Struggle for Justice in the 21st Century*. Berkeley: University of California Press, 2008.

Sherman, Rachel. *Class Acts: Service and Inequality in Luxury Hotels*. Berkeley: University of California Press, 2007.

Snow, David A., and Robert D. Benford. "Clarifying the Relationship between Framing and Ideology." *Mobilization* 5:1 (2000): 55–60.

Snow, David A., E. Burke Rochford Jr., Steven K. Worden, and Robert D. Benford. "Frame Alignment Processes, Micromobilization, and Movement Participation." *American Sociological Review* 51:4 (1986): 464–81.

Steinberg, Marc. "The Talk and Back Talk of Collective Action: A Dialogic Analysis of Repertoires of Discourse among Nineteenth-Century Cotton Spinners." *American Journal of Sociology* 105:3 (1999): 736–80.

——. "Tilting the Frame: Framing from a Discursive Turn." *Sociological Theory* 27:6 (1998): 845–72.

Stepan-Norris, Judith, and Caleb Southworth. "Rival Unionism and Membership Growth: A Special Case of Inter-Organizational Competition." *American Sociological Review* 75:2 (2010): 227–51.

Stern, Andy. *A Country That Works: Getting America Back on Track*. New York: Free Press, 2006.

Stevens, Rosemary. *American Medicine and the Public Interest: A History of Specialization*. New Haven: Yale University Press, 1971.

——. *In Sickness and in Wealth: American Hospitals in the Twentieth Century*. New York: Basic Books, 1989.

Stevenson, David, and David Studdert. "The Rise of Nursing Home Litigation: Findings from a National Survey of Attorneys." *Health Affairs* 22:2 (2003): 219–29.

Studdert, David, and David Stevenson. "Nursing Home Litigation and Tort Reform: A Case for 'Exceptionalism.'" *Gerontologist* 44:5 (2004): 588–95.

Thompson, Margaret. "Discovering Foremothers: Sisters, Society, and the American Catholic Experience." *U.S. Catholic Historian* 5 (1986): 273–90.

Thompson, Stephen L., and J. Warren Salmon. "Physician Collective Bargaining in a U.S. Public Hospital." *International Journal of Health Services* 33:1 (2003): 55–76.

Tolich, Martin B. "Alienating and Liberating Emotions at Work: Supermarket Clerks' Performance of Customer Service." *Journal of Contemporary Ethnography* 22:3 (1993): 361–81.

United States Conference of Catholic Bishops. *A Fair and Just Workplace: Principles and Practices for Catholic Health Care.* Washington, D.C., 1999.

Useem, Michael. *The Inner Circle: Large Corporations and the Rise of Business Political Activity in the US and UK.* New York: Oxford University Press, 1984.

Uzzi, Brian. "The Sources and Consequences of Embeddedness for the Economic Performance of Organizations: The Network Effect." *American Journal of Sociology* 61:4 (1996): 674–98.

Voss, Kim, and Rachel Sherman. "Breaking the Iron Law of Oligarchy: Union Revitalization in the American Labor Movement." *American Journal of Sociology* 106:2 (2000): 303–49.

Wall, Barbra Mann. *American Catholic Hospitals: A Century of Changing Markets and Missions.* New Brunswick, N.J.: Rutgers University Press, 2011.

———. *Unlikely Entrepreneurs: Catholic Sisters and the Hospital Marketplace, 1865–1925.* Columbus: Ohio State University Press, 2005.

Warren, Mark R. *Dry Bones Rattling: Community Building to Revitalize America's Democracy.* Princeton, N.J.: Princeton University Press, 2001.

Weinbaum, Eve, and Gordon Lafer. "Outside Agitators and Other Red Herrings: Getting Past the 'Top-Down/Bottom-Up' Debate." *New Labor Forum* 10 (2002): 26–35.

Western, Bruce. *Between Class and Market: Postwar Unionization in the Capitalist Democracies.* Princeton, N.J.: Princeton University Press, 1997.

White, Kenneth R. "Hospitals Sponsored by the Roman Catholic Church: Separate, Equal, and Distinct?" *Milbank Quarterly* 78:2 (2000): 213–39.

Wilson, William Julius. *The Truly Disadvantaged: The Inner City, The Underclass, and Public Policy.* Chicago: University of Chicago Press, 1987.

Winslow, Cal. *Labor's Civil War in California: The NUHW Healthcare Workers' Rebellion.* Oakland, Calif.: PM Press, 2010.

Wunnava, Phanindra V., and Noga O. Peled. "Union Wage Premiums by Gender and Race: Evidence from PSID 1980–1992." *Journal of Labor Research* 20:3 (1999): 415–23.

Zelizer, Viviana. "The Social Meaning of Money: 'Special Monies.'" *American Journal of Sociology* 95:2 (1989): 342–77.

INDEX

Page numbers in *italics* refer to figures.